Language
for Learning

Also available

Word Play
Language Activities for Young Children
Sheila Wolfendale and Trevor Bryans
978-1-84312-439-9

Soundaround
Developing Phonological Awareness Skills in the Foundation Stage
Andrew Burnett and Jackie Wylie
978-1-84312-001-8

Developing Speech and Language Skills (Phoneme Factory)
Gwen Lancaster
978-1-84312-382-8

Chataway
Developing Speech and Language Skills
Andrew Burnett and Jackie Wylie
978-1-84312-438-2

Language
for Learning

a practical guide for supporting
pupils with language and
communication difficulties
across the curriculum

Sue Hayden and Emma Jordan

LONDON AND NEW YORK

Routledge
2 Park Square, Milton Park, Abingdon, Oxon OX414 4RN

Simultaneously published in the USA and Canada
by Routledge
270 Madison Ave, New York, NY 10016

First published in 2004 by Language for Learning, Kidderminster
This edition published 2007 by Routledge in association with the National Association for Special
Educational Needs (NASEN)

NASEN is a registered charity no. 1007023.

Routledge is an imprint of the Taylor & Francis Group, an informa business

Illustrations by Jacqui Bignell

Typeset in Goudy by Servis Filmsetting, Manchester & FiSH Books, London
Printed and bound in India

British Library Cataloguing in Publication Data
A catalogue record for this book is available from the British Library.

Library of Congress Cataloging in Publication Data
A catalogue record has been requested.

ISBN 10: 1-84312-468-8
ISBN 13: 978-1-84312-468-9

Contents

Contents

nasen is a professional membership association which supports all those who work with or care for children and young people with special and additional educational needs. Members include teachers, teaching assistants, support workers, other educationalists, students and parents.

nasen supports its members through policy documents, journals, its magazine *Special!*, publications, professional development courses, regional networks and newsletters. Its website contains more current information such as responses to government consultations. **nasen**'s published documents are held in very high regard both in the UK and internationally.

Acknowledgements

We would like to thank our colleagues from the Access and Inclusion: Learning Support Team and the Wyre Forest Speech and Language Therapy Service for their continual support and encouragement.

We would also like to thank:

Chris Green, Jackie Tubb, Irene Punt and June Seymour for their professional advice and guidance; the Language for Learning Strategic Group for their kind permission to reproduce illustrations within the book taken from the Language for Learning resources;

Our Language for Learning trainers who generously shared their knowledge, skills and practical ideas;

Maggie Johnson who originally brought inspiration to Worcestershire through the Functional Communication training courses; and

Elaine Packwood and Pamela Connolly for their administrative support and help.

Introduction

The first edition of this book, *Language for Learning Across the Curriculum*, was based upon *Speaking and Listening: Stage One* and *Speaking and Listening: Stage Two* (Hayden 1996). Since writing the original books in 1996, Sue Hayden has worked in partnership with Emma Jordan to develop the 'Language for Learning' project.

Language for Learning is a joint health and education project providing a collaborative approach to training those working with children who have speech, language or communication difficulties. Since April 2000, a range of training courses has been developed to support inclusion of children with language and communication difficulties across all stages of the curriculum – from Foundation Stage to Key Stage 4.

This book has been developed to provide a practical guide for practitioners supporting pupils with speech, language and/or communication difficulties across Key Stages 1 & 2 in mainstream settings.

It aims to support inclusive practice by helping readers to understand how language is processed; to identify speech, language and communication difficulties; to support the development of skills across meaningful learning opportunities; and to empower pupils to access the curriculum.

For ease of reference, areas of language have been both colour and symbol coded throughout the book. Stickers of these coloured symbols are provided to link school resources and activity ideas with each area of language.

A Framework for Supporting Pupils with Speech, Language and Communication Difficulties

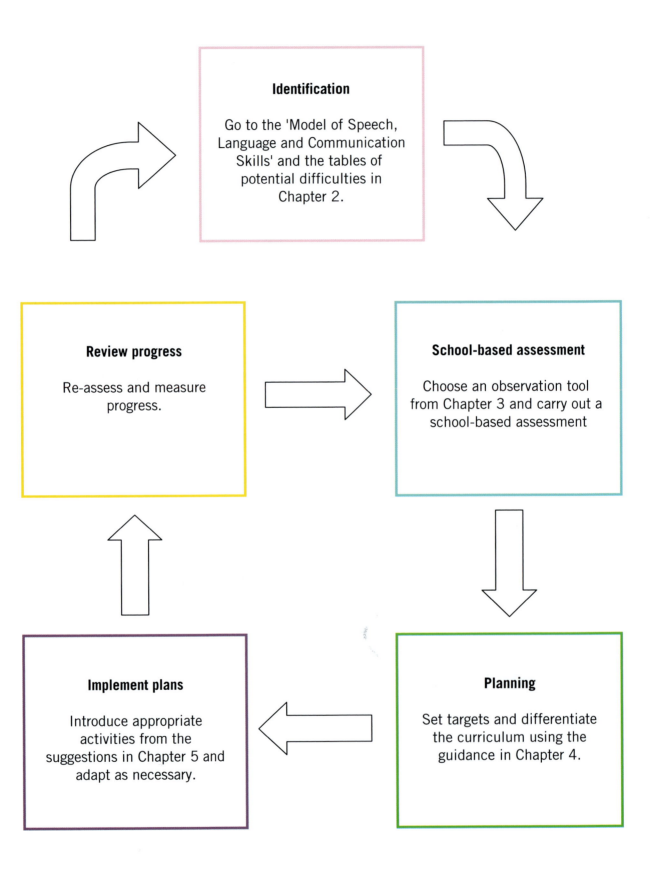

Identification

Go to the 'Model of Speech, Language and Communication Skills' and the tables of potential difficulties in Chapter 2.

School-based assessment

Choose an observation tool from Chapter 3 and carry out a school-based assessment

Planning

Set targets and differentiate the curriculum using the guidance in Chapter 4.

Implement plans

Introduce appropriate activities from the suggestions in Chapter 5 and adapt as necessary.

Review progress

Re-assess and measure progress.

Key to Symbols

	Attention and Listening Skills	Hearing, vision, attention, listening, motivation
	Understanding the Meaning of Words	Vocabulary store Meaning of words and sentences
	Structure & Rules	Speech sound system Sentence construction skills
	Social Communication Skills	Desire to communicate Social use of language Conversational skills
	Working Auditory Memory	Remembering what has been said/what needs to be said when processing language
	Speech	Articulation Producing speech sounds

Language and Communication

This chapter describes the language skills required to access the curriculum and socialise appropriately in school. A theoretical model of speech, language and communication skills is presented.

It aims to provide practitioners with an understanding of speech, language and communication skills and a shared language to talk about language.

Speech, language and communication difficulties are described in order to help practitioners to identify needs in the classroom.

A Model of Speech, Language and Communication Skills

Understanding and using language is a complicated process. It is important for practitioners to use a framework or model for thinking and talking about speech, language and communication skills.

The Model of Speech, Language and Communication Skills on p.8 provides this framework. The boxes on the model represent areas of language:

Desire to Communicate

This social communication skill is an innate skill which is fundamental to language and communication development. Communication happens for social purposes, not just to meet personal needs. Children need an idea to communicate and an opportunity to do so.

Attention, Listening, Hearing, Vision and Motivation

The ability to hear what someone has said, see the non-verbal clues or body language used, attend to the speaker and be interested in what the speaker has to say.

Understanding the Meaning of Words

The ability to understand and use concepts, words and sentences. This is the vocabulary store or the 'semantic system', which stores word meanings, associations and links words together by category.

Structure and Rules

Language is governed by a set of rules and is structured in a specific way. Skills in this area include:

- Phonology – the speech sound storage system; rules governing how sounds are combined to form words.
- Syntax – the way in which words are combined to form sentences and narratives; the rules governing word order.
- Morphology – changes made to the beginnings and endings of words to alter the meaning, for instance, walk – walk<u>ing</u> – walk<u>ed</u> – walk<u>s.</u>

Social Communication Skills

The ability to use language skills in social situations. Skills in this area include conversational skills, such as turn-taking and topic maintenance; and non-verbal skills, such as the use of eye contact and facial expression.

Working Auditory Memory

This is the ability to remember information for a sufficient period of time in order to process it and to understand its meaning. It also allows speakers to remember what has been said and what still needs to be said.

Speech

The ability to co-ordinate the mouth to produce the sounds to make words.

A Model to Represent Speech, Language and Communication Skills

Desire to Communicate

An idea to express and the opportunity to express it

Understanding the Meaning of Words

- Concepts
- Words – vocabulary and word meaning
- Sentences – meaning of whole sentences

BIG
GROSS
GIGANTIC
ENORMOUS
HUGE
TALL

Structure & Rules

- Sound combinations to form words
- Word combinations to form sentences
- Sentences to form narratives

Social Communication Skills

- Conversational skills
- Non-verbal skills – gesture, body language, facial expression, eye contact
- Proximity/distance

Working Auditory Memory

- Remembering what has been said/what needs to be said when processing language

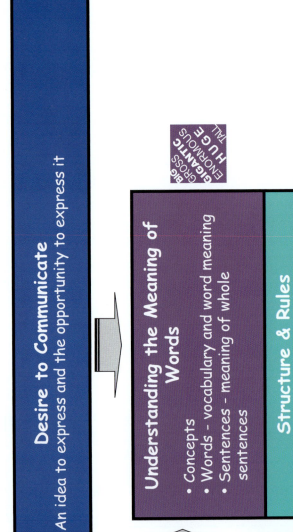

Attention & Listening

- Hearing
- Vision
- Attention control
- Motivation

Speech

- Move mouth to form sounds and produce words

Receptive and Expressive Language

In order to understand language, i.e. receptive language, the following route is taken:

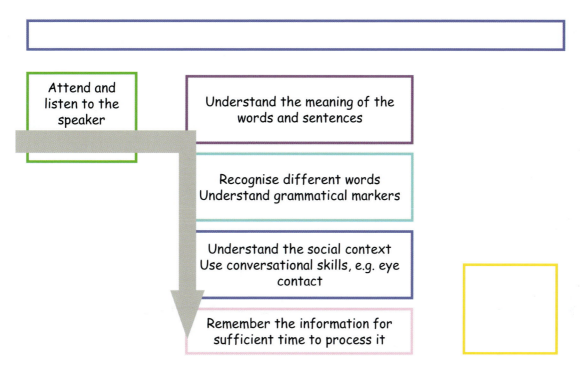

In order to use language, i.e. expressive language, the following route is taken:

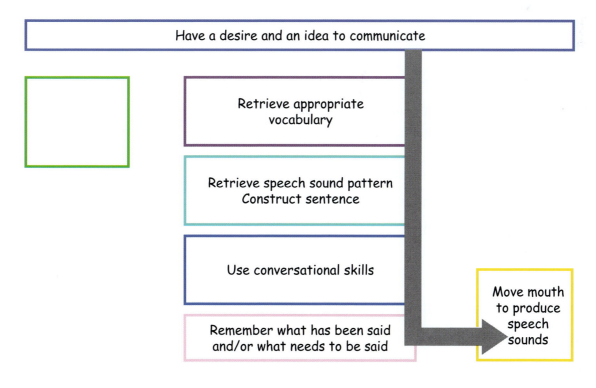

Speech, Language and Communication Difficulties

The ability to understand and use language underpins access to all areas of the curriculum. Pupils need to be able to listen; follow instructions; use appropriate vocabulary; construct sentences; and use language for social purposes in order to succeed both academically and socially in school. However, research suggests that at least three pupils in every class (Law *et al.* 2000) will at some point experience speech, language or communication difficulties.

The recent introduction of the Speaking, Listening and Learning Curriculum (DfES 2004) within the National Primary Strategy has highlighted the importance of developing language and communication skills. However this curriculum brings additional challenges for pupils with speech and language difficulties.

A collaborative approach – one that involves teachers, teaching/learning support assistants, parents/carers, speech and language therapists, specialist teachers and educational psychologists – is vital to ensure that pupils' needs are met effectively in their school setting. This type of approach has been supported within the literature (Speake 2003; Ripley, Barrett and Fleming 2001; Martin 2000) and by recent legislation (DfES 2001a). The role of the speech and language therapist in education settings has also become clearer (DfES 2001b). Early identification of difficulties can help to prevent secondary problems with the development of social, emotional and academic skills.

Initial Identification

Pupils with speech, language and/or communication difficulties often present with a range of difficulties in the classroom, for instance:

- Attention and listening difficulties
- Problems remembering instructions
- Difficulties making themselves understood
- Being the last to complete work
- Immature vocabulary development
- Difficulties making friends
- Being non-compliant
- Giving strange or unusual responses to questions

The context, i.e. different people and places, will also impact upon a pupil's skills. Some pupils may be able to understand and use language skills in one situation but not another.

The school environment and the National Curriculum bring another set of demands – the use of **language for learning** not just communicating; new vocabulary; new situations; and new people. As a result of this, the majority of pupils with speech or language difficulties find school challenging.

Types of Difficulties

Pupils may experience difficulties in the following areas:

Delayed Speech and Language Skills

An increasing number of children are entering school with delayed speech and language skills. In areas of social deprivation this number is even higher. Pupils with delayed skills often have immature development in most/all areas of language.

Potential difficulties	Area
Attention skills Listening skills Processing of auditory information	
Vocabulary development – understanding and use of single word vocabulary Lack of exposure to language Concept development	
Understanding and use of grammar Phonological skills	
Understanding social rules Using language in social situations Turn-taking skills Awareness of other people and ability to interact with peers	
Working auditory memory	
Articulation	

Receptive Language Difficulties

This refers to difficulties 'receiving' language, i.e. processing language and understanding the meaning of language. Pupils with receptive language difficulties are often able to mask problems of understanding in the classroom by copying their peers; using visual information; familiar routines; and non-verbal signals to support their understanding. It does not necessarily follow that a child with good expressive skills or use of language has good receptive skills.

Potential difficulties	Area
Attention and listening skills	
Vocabulary development – understanding of single word vocabulary Concept development	
Understanding and use of grammar	
Understanding non-literal or ambiguous language	
Working auditory memory	

Expressive Language Difficulties

Difficulties developing vocabulary; using language in meaningful sentences; and constructing sentences using grammatical knowledge/skills. Often these difficulties are easily identifiable as the pupil's language may appear immature, their choice of vocabulary may be limited and sentences may be disjointed or incomplete.

Potential difficulties	Area
Vocabulary development – use of single word vocabulary Word retrieval skills Using both concrete and abstract language	
Sentence construction skills Use of grammar	

Specific Language Difficulties

Some pupils experience specific language difficulties, i.e. a specific difficulty with language. For instance, some pupils may experience specific difficulties developing their understanding of the meaning of words, i.e. a specific semantic difficulty. These difficulties are often difficult to identify and pupils will need specialist assessment by a speech and language therapist or specialist teacher.

Potential difficulties	Area
Vocabulary development – understanding and use of single word vocabulary Concept development	
Understanding and use of grammar	
Understanding social rules Using language effectively in social situations	

Speech Sound Difficulties

Pupils may experience difficulties developing and using speech sounds. This may be because of a difficulty storing sounds within the phonological system or in actually articulating sounds. These children should be identified easily as their speech may be difficult to understand, particularly out of context.

Potential difficulties	Area
Phonological skills	
Articulation	

Associated Difficulties

Some children experience speech, language and communication difficulties in association with another difficulty.

Sensory Impairments

Indicators of Hearing Loss

Physical	• history of ear infections
	• frequent colds and coughs
	• complaints of earache
	• breathing through mouth
	• catarrhal
	• discharge from ears
Behavioural	• daydreams
	• tires easily
	• is listless
	• is irritable
	• is withdrawn – shows little interaction
Functional	• volume of speech noticeably loud/quiet
	• has unclear speech
	• uses limited vocabulary
	• responds slowly to instructions
	• responds inappropriately
	• constantly asks for repetition
	• turns head to locate sound
	• cannot function in noisy conditions
	• relies on facial or lip clues
	• omits some word endings
	• has weak phonic skills

Fluctuating Hearing Loss

This is very common in primary-age children, occurring when a wax plug presses against the ear-drum, or infection of the upper respiratory tract spreads to the middle ear (otitis media), causing spasmodic deafness and ongoing auditory interference. Fluctuating hearing loss can be difficult to assess as a child's hearing levels can vary greatly over a short period of time.

Potential difficulties	Area
Attention control Processing of auditory information Distracted by background noise	
Discrimination between similar sounds Phonological skills	
Articulation	

Sensori-neural Hearing Loss

Between two and three children in every 5,000 experience a sensori-neural hearing loss. The nerve pathways to the brain are permanently affected, causing mild to profound deafness. Both receptive and expressive language may be affected. These children may be exposed to a signing environment and to the different social rules practised by the deaf community.

Potential difficulties	Area
Attention skills Processing of auditory information	
Vocabulary development – use of single word Concept development	
Understanding and use of grammar Phonological skills	
Fine tuning of language according to context Understanding social rules Awareness of other people Turn-taking skills	
Articulation	

Visual Impairment

Visual difficulties can range from very mild, corrected by glasses or exercises, to severe conditions that warrant a Statement of Special Educational Needs. Often visual impairment, which could affect other areas of development, is not detected until paper and pencil skills are being developed.

Potential difficulties	Area
Following instructions supported by non-verbal clues	
Ability to recognise objects and name Understanding associations between words Sorting and classifying skills Descriptive skills Awareness of gender and the use of pronouns Using 'this', 'that', 'here' and 'there' Interpretation of verbs Use of visual terms/concepts Use of prepositions and the concept of space	
Rhyming and rhythmic skills	
Interpretation and understanding of gesture Ability to secure adult's/peer's attention Role play and imitation skills	
Recognition of mouth shapes to make sounds	

Neurodevelopmental Difficulties

Autism Spectrum Conditions (ASC)

Children with an autism spectrum disorder, i.e. autism, Asperger's Syndrome or semantic pragmatic disorder, experience difficulties within the 'triad of impairments'. The triad includes social interaction, social communication and flexibility of thought.

Potential difficulties	Area
Attention and listening control Processing information Filtering information and deciding what is redundant	
Understanding the meaning of words Use of sophisticated vocabulary without meaning Understanding associations between words Sorting and classifying skills Word-finding skills Descriptive skills Understanding words with multiple meanings Reading for meaning	
Use of language for social purposes Turn-taking skills Maintaining a topic of conversation Use of eye contact Use of appropriate proximity/distance Understanding cause and effect in social situations Understanding non-verbal means of communication Understanding and using non-literal or ambiguous language	

Attention Deficit Hyperactivity Disorder (ADHD)

Children experiencing ADHD find it difficult to focus and maintain their attention. They are likely to experience difficulties with cause and effect in social situations; understanding social cues and maintaining attention and listening skills within lesson time. They experience difficulties applying rules in social situations.

Potential difficulties	Area
Attention control Focusing on the speaker Listening skills	
Understanding associations between words Sorting and classifying skills	
Turn-taking skills Maintaining a topic of conversation Use of eye contact Recognition of facial expressions Understanding cause and effect	

Physical Factors

Structural Problems

Children born with structural problems, such as cleft lip or palate or children who have suffered injuries to the head, face or mouth often have subsequent speech and language difficulties. This may be due to possible Eustachian tube malfunction and/or the inability to manoeuvre the vocal tract.

Potential difficulties	Area
Listening difficulties Ability to follow instructions	
Use of facial expression Use of eye contact	
Articulation	

Cerebral Palsy

Children with cerebral palsy may experience associated language and learning difficulties.

Potential difficulties	Area
Attention control Listening difficulties Ability to follow instructions	
Understanding concrete and abstract concepts Sorting and classifying skills	
Use of facial expression Use of eye contact Understanding social rules	
Articulation	

Psychological Factors

Anxiety

Children experiencing temporary or permanent feelings of anxiety or great emotional trauma often respond in ways that affect their language or communication skills.

Potential difficulties	Area
Selective mutism Use of eye contact Avoidance of verbal responses	
Stammering	

Emotional Deprivation

Delayed speech and language can be caused by emotional and/or physical deprivation or neglect. The development of early language skills is hampered by the lack of caring, individual adult/child interaction and a safe environment in which to explore.

Potential difficulties	Area
Attention control	
Vocabulary development is restricted Understanding abstract concepts	
Use of eye contact Turn-taking skills Understanding social rules and situations	

Learning Difficulties

Specific Learning Difficulties (SpLD)

Pupils who have difficulty in acquiring skills in specific areas – usually reading, numeracy and organisation – are often articulate and enjoy talking. There can, however, be difficulty with the language of sequencing, auditory discrimination, auditory memory, classifying and sorting.

Potential difficulties	Area
Word-finding skills Sorting and classifying skills Use of prepositions, pronouns, adverbs and adjectives	
Following instructions requiring sequencing skills Auditory discrimination Rhyming and rhythmic skills Phonic skills	
Working auditory memory	

21

Moderate Learning Difficulties

Children with moderate learning difficulties have delayed speech and language skills.	
Potential difficulties	**Area**
Attention control Listening	
Understanding vocabulary and abstract concepts Use of prepositions, pronouns, adverbs and adjectives Sorting and classifying skills	
Understanding instructions Knowledge of tenses Use of plurals, possessives and pronouns Phonological skills Rhyming and rhythmic skills	
Working auditory memory	
Articulation	

Environmental Factors

Developing a Second Language

A young child in full-time education does not usually have a problem acquiring a second language, provided that cognitive skills, hearing, speech and social skills are developing typically. It may be necessary to carry out an assessment in his/her first language if there is uncertainty about language development. Some cultures discourage eye contact, particularly amongst girls.

Potential difficulties	Area
Attention control Processing of auditory information	
Vocabulary development	
Understanding and use of English grammatical structures	
Understanding social rules and cultural differences Use of eye contact Turn-taking skills	

Large Family

This is usually a good environment for language development, but if a child has one or more of the difficulties associated with speech, language or communication, he/she may be hampered by the constant background noise, others anticipating his/her needs, and lack of individual attention.

Potential difficulties	Area
Listening skills	
Vocabulary development Descriptive skills	
Ability to formulate and answer questions	
Articulation	

Twins

Twins can have special problems related to language as they may develop their own code or may be so self contained that they do not feel the need to communicate with others.

Potential difficulties	Area
Attention control Listening skills	
Vocabulary development	
Sentence-construction skills Phonological difficulties	
Awareness of context and other people	

Deaf Parents

A hearing child of deaf parents may experience many problems that are not obvious. Natural speech sounds are not heard frequently. Social communication is affected by the different social rules practised by the deaf community. See also 'Sensori-neural Hearing Loss' as similar difficulties may occur.

Potential difficulties	Area
Listening skills Processing of auditory information	
Vocabulary development – understanding and use of single word vocabulary Concept development	
Understanding and use of grammar Phonological difficulties	
Understanding social rules Understanding non-literal or ambiguous language	
Working auditory memory	
Articulation	

General Factors

Our changing lifestyle has reduced the amount of time we spend conversing with each other face to face. Children listen to half conversations on telephones. The television, which is often on in the background, has chairs arranged to face it, rather than each other, so attention is not fully on the speaker. Mothers feed babies whilst watching television, denying them the shared mutual gaze and non-verbal facial awareness necessary for early language development. Shopping is no longer a sociable occupation: the language of requesting, describing, choosing, etc., is now redundant in large supermarkets. There is an increasing reliance on visual communication.

Potential difficulties	Area
Attention control Listening skills Processing of auditory information	
Vocabulary development Concept development	
Understanding and use of grammar	
Understanding social rules and situations Use of eye contact Awareness of other people Turn-taking skills	
Working auditory memory	

3 Identifying Strengths and Needs

This chapter provides a guide to school based assessment and identification of speech, language and communication difficulties.

A collaborative approach is essential when assessing speech, language and communication skills. As highlighted in Chapter 2, a pupil's skills may vary greatly from one situation to another, so it is important for all agencies to work together in order to gain a holistic picture of the pupil's needs. This chapter provides a range of assessment tools that will support collaborative assessment.

Observation is a powerful tool and therefore forms the basis of all assessments within this chapter. Observing the pupil both at home and at school will provide valuable information about his or her strengths and needs.

Observation

Observation can provide a wealth of information about a pupil's speech, language and communication skills across a range of contexts. It can also help to identify the impact of the pupil's difficulty on the development of social interaction and relationships with both peers and adults. Observation can highlight potential areas of difficulty across the curriculum and environmental factors that may be affecting a pupil's understanding or use of language.

It is useful to carry out observations in both structured and unstructured situations across different areas of the curriculum, for instance during playtime, during PSHE or Circle Time, and during literacy or numeracy.

Often practitioners have invaluable information about a pupil gained through everyday observations. However, this information may not be recorded or shared in a formal way. It is essential to record observations in order to establish a baseline, to identify strengths and needs and to measure progress.

Tips for Observation

- Remember that observation is more than just watching (Tilstone 1998). It involves the collection of information, making sense of the findings and then drawing conclusions.

- Consider the context:
  - Location, e.g. classroom, playground, hall.
  - Type of activity, e.g. lesson, free play, discussion, lunch.
  - Teaching situation, e.g. whole class, small group, individual.

- Think about how the information will be recorded:
  - Nudge sheet with key words that act as a reminder.
  - A specific observation tool.
  - Consider confidentiality, professionalism, tact and objectivity.

- Work together to achieve a holistic picture:
  - Agree when and where the observations will take place.
  - Identify both strengths and needs.
  - Consider all areas of language.
  - Agree how the information will be shared.

- Reflect on findings:
  - Share findings as a team and work towards developing a shared understanding of the nature of the pupil's difficulties.
  - Record findings on the Model of Speech, Language and Communication Skills described in Chapter 2.
  - Identify what to do next.
  - Set targets and choose appropriate strategies and activities as suggested in Chapter 5.

Observation-based Assessment Tools

The assessment tools provided in this chapter have been designed for use by practitioners in schools. They are quick and easy to complete and will lead directly to target setting and strategy planning.

The first three assessment tools are based upon the areas of language identified in the previous chapter.

1 The 'Whole Class Observations' tool on pp. 30–31 provides practitioners with the opportunity to record information about a number of pupils within a class. As difficulties are observed, the practitioner records pupils' names and can begin to identify pupils of concern. This tool also enables practitioners to group pupils for targeted small group work.

2 The 'Quick Observation Based Assessment: Speech, Language and Communication Skills' on pp. 32–34 will remind practitioners of specific areas of language to observe and consider. It is simple to complete – by using existing knowledge of the pupil, the practitioner works through each area of language answering each question by ticking the yes/no column and adding any additional comments. Ticks in the 'no' column suggest potential areas of difficulty.

3 The 'Observation Sheet' on p. 35 can be used by practitioners observing a pupil within a specific situation or context. A profile can be formed by recording areas of strength and need within each area of language.

4 The 'Developmental Chart' on p. 36 provides information about the approximate age of development of a number of skills – understanding language; use of language; use of speech sounds; attention control; social behaviour; and play skills. This can be useful when trying to establish if a pupil is experiencing a general speech and language delay or a specific difficulty.

When the assessment has been completed, refer to Chapter 5 for strategy, activity and resource ideas for whole class, small group and individual teaching.

1. Whole Class Observations

Language Areas	Observations	Names
ATTENTION AND LISTENING SKILLS	• Difficulties sitting still during whole class teaching	
	• Focuses attention very briefly	
	• Does not respond when whole class asked to listen	
	• Instructions need to be simplified in order to be understood	
	• Does not comply with instructions	
	• Does not ask for clarification	
	• Difficulties staying on task	
UNDERSTANDING THE MEANING OF WORDS	• Difficulties understanding new vocabulary	
	• Limited use of vocabulary	
	• Word finding difficulties	
	• Difficulties understanding and using abstract concepts	
	• Difficulties responding to question words	
	• Difficulties defining words or making links between words	
	• Problems reading for meaning	
STRUCTURE AND RULES: SYNTAX	• Difficulties constructing sentences	
	• Uses immature sentences	
	• Uses the wrong tense	
	• Uses telegrammatic sentences, i.e. only uses key words	
	• Puts words in the wrong order	
	• Uses the wrong word endings	
	• Misunderstands negatives, pronouns, plurals and/or tenses	

Language Areas		Observations	Names
STRUCTURE AND RULES: PHONOLOGY		• Unintelligible speech	
		• Difficulties blending sounds	
		• Substitutes or misses sounds from words	
		• Difficulties with phonological awareness activities	
SOCIAL COMMUNICATION SKILLS		• Difficulties taking turns or using eye contact	
		• Makes irrelevant comments or asks inappropriate questions	
		• Interrupts/changes the topic of conversation rapidly	
		• Uses inappropriate volume, intonation or unusual voice	
		• Laughs at the wrong time, appears cheeky/rude	
		• Tends to talk at people rather than to them	
		• May take the adult role	
		• Difficulties understanding ambiguous language	
WORKING AUDITORY MEMORY		• Forgets instructions	
		• Gets lost within an activity	
		• Appears non-compliant	
		• Is unable to recall information or instructions	
		• Repeats him/herself	
SPEECH		• Difficulties producing speech sounds	
		• Speech deteriorates when excited or nervous	
		• Syllables in polysyllabic words are left out	

2. Quick Observation-based Assessment
Speech, Language and Communication Skills

Name:	Age:	Date:
Practitioner:	Year Group:	Review Date:

AREA OF LANGUAGE	YES	NO	COMMENTS
Attention and Listening			
1. Does he/she demonstrate appropriate attention and listening skills during: • Individual work with adult or peer • Small group work • Whole class work			
2. Does he/she ask for clarification?			
3. Does he/she respond appropriately to instructions during: • Small group work • Whole class situations			
4. Does he/she respond appropriately to: • Instructions • Questions • Stories • Discussions/general conversations			
Understanding the Meaning of Words			
5. Does he/she understand and use a range of vocabulary, i.e. nouns, verbs, adjectives?			
6. Is he/she able to learn and use new vocabulary appropriately?			
7. Is he/she able to understand and use abstract concepts?			
8. Does he/she respond appropriately to questions?			
9. Is he/she able to define familiar words?			

AREA OF LANGUAGE	YES	NO	COMMENTS
Structure and Rules: Syntax			35
10. Is he/she able to construct sentences using appropriate grammar (e.g. pronouns, tenses, conjunctions)?			
11. Does he/she use the correct word order when constructing sentences?			
12. Does he/she respond appropriately to: • Instructions • Stories			
Structure and Rules: Phonology			
13. Is he/she intelligible?			
14. Is he/she substituting sounds persistently, e.g. using 't' for 'k'?			
15. Is he/she experiencing difficulties acquiring phonological awareness skills during literacy?			
Social Communication Skills			
16. Does the pupil use his/her language skills for a number of reasons, e.g. to request, to comment, to greet, to suggest, to negotiate?			
17. Is he/she able to initiate and continue a conversation?			
18. Is he/she able to terminate a conversation appropriately?			
19. Does he/she take turns in a conversation?			
20. Does he/she stay on topic?			
21. Does he/she use appropriate eye contact?			
22. Does he/she understand and use non-verbal means of communication, e.g. facial expressions, gesture?			

AREA OF LANGUAGE	YES	NO	COMMENTS
Social Communication Skills			
23. Does he/she provide the listener with sufficient information to understand?			
24. Does he/she respond appropriately to ambiguous language, such as metaphors, similes or jokes?			
Working Auditory Memory Skills			
25. Does he/she remember what has been said within: • Instructions • Stories			
26. Does he/she repeat him/herself when using language, for instance when giving news or telling a story ?			
Speech			
27. Is he/she able to produce speech sounds accurately?			

3. Observation Sheet

Name:	Age:	Year Group:
Observer:		Date:

Description of Activity:

OBSERVATIONS

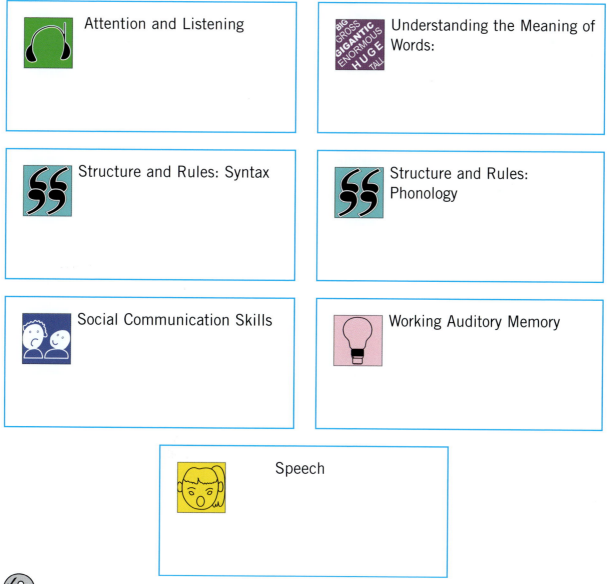

Attention and Listening

Understanding the Meaning of Words:

Structure and Rules: Syntax

Structure and Rules: Phonology

Social Communication Skills

Working Auditory Memory

Speech

4. Developmental Chart

Age	Understanding of Language	Use of Language
0 months → 6 months	• Turns towards sounds • Responds to intonation patterns	• Uses voice and/or body movement
12 months	• Understands short phrases when part of a familiar routine	• Babbles • Begins to express a range of first meanings by gesture and vocalisation, e.g. requesting, rejecting, greeting
18 months	• Situational understanding, i.e. understands key words in familiar, concrete situations	• Uses voice to imitate • Uses facial expressions • Uses single words
2 years	• Understands single words consistently, e.g. find your <u>coat</u>	• More recognisable single words • Occasionally puts two words together, e.g. all gone
3 years	• Understands two key word sentences, e.g. put your <u>train</u> in the <u>box</u> • Identifies functions of familiar objects, e.g. what do you drink from? • Begins to understand abstract concepts, e.g. size and colour • Understands prepositions and negatives • Begins to develop the concept of time	• Uses an extended vocabulary of concrete and abstract words • Puts two or three key word sentences together • Starts to use questions • Learns rhymes
4 years	• Understand three key word sentences • Extends understanding of abstract concepts	• Uses four word sentences • Uses 'and' to link ideas • Uses pronouns, e.g. 'I' and regular plurals • Chats to others during play • Begins to take turns
5 years	• Follows simple stories • Shows greater concentration when listening	• Uses negatives, pronouns, prepositions and past tenses in four to five word sentences • Names, predicts and describes objects and situations • Vocabulary of approximately 5,000 words • Retells stories

Speech Sounds	Attention Control	Social Behaviour and Play Skills
	• Very little attention control • Distracted by every visual and auditory stimulus	• Looks towards adult's face

• Uses
  p,b,t,d
  m,n
  w
• Misses ends of words
		• Friendly with strangers, begins to show signs of anxiety if mother out of sight
		• Takes everything to mouth, reaches for things out of sight

		• Enjoys making sounds with rattles/bells • Enjoys giving and receiving objects • Initiates simple games like hiding toys
	• Single channelled attention	• Some understanding of common danger • Engages in make-believe situations • Unable to share, plays in parallel

• Uses:
  p,b,t,d,k,g
  m,n,ng
  f,s
  w,j,h
	• Still single channelled attention
	• With adult help, will stop what he/she is doing, listen or look at something else and then return to original task
		• Beginning to share and engage in integrated play with other children
		• Shows affection and enjoys helping
		• Can invent people and objects in make-believe play
		• Beginning to accept that needs may not be met immediately

• Uses:
  p,b,t,d,k,g
  m,n,ng
  f,v,s,z,sh,ch,j
  w,l,j,h
	• Will attend to speaker without adult help, but possible to continue the task at the same time as listening	• More independent and strong willed
		• Often quarrels with adults and other children, but is beginning to realise that this should be verbal and not physical
		• Can share and take turns
		• Shows concerns for others

• Uses:
  p,b,t,d,k,g
  m,n,ng
  f,v,s,z,sh,ch,j
  w,l,j,h,r
	• Two channelled attention – can listen and do at the same time
	• Short attention span, but can be taught in small groups
		• Developing 'theory of mind'
		• Plays well with peers both imaginatively and structurally
		• Understands the need for rules and fair play
		• Has definite sense of humour
		• Looks after younger children and animals

4 Supporting Pupils to Access the National Curriculum

The National Curriculum provides guidelines to develop speaking and listening skills. This chapter helps practitioners to make the link between this legislation and classroom practice when supporting pupils with speech, language and communication difficulties.

The first section looks at the teaching objectives through the *National Curriculum's Programmes of Study* and *Primary Strategy for Speaking, Listening and Learning*, and the second at *Scales of Performance (P-Scales)* and *Attainment Targets*.

The first set of tables (pp. 42–65) marry the broad teaching objectives of the *Programmes of Study for English 1* (Speaking and Listening) of the National Curriculum to the specific teaching objectives of the *Primary Strategy for Speaking, Listening and Learning* (Speaking and Listening Strands only). The skills pupils need in order to meet both sets of objectives are identified. Finally, specific strategies from Chapter 5 are suggested for the development of each skill.

The second set of tables (pp. 66–77) looks at the progression of skills through the P-Scales and the Attainment Targets.

The National Curriculum

The National Curriculum's Programme of Study (QCA 1999) outline the four main speaking and listening *strands*, the *objectives* and the *skills* to be developed. The *objectives* are set out in broad terms whereas the *skills* are specific.

The Primary Strategy for Speaking, Listening and Learning (DfES/QCA 2003) refers to the same four speaking and listening *strands* and describes the *objectives* in more detail.

The following section takes the *strands* and the *objectives* from both documents and the *skills* from the *Programme of Study* and links them to an extensive range of practical strategies in Chapter 5.

Key Stage 1 Strand One: Speaking

Broad Objectives *Programmes of Study*	Specific Objectives *Primary Strategy: Speaking, Listening and Learning*	Skills
SPEAKING Speaks clearly, fluently and confidently to different people	**Year 1 Term 1** 1. Describe incidents/tell stories from own experience in an audible voice	Stays on topic
		Expresses feelings
		Has basic grammar
		Speaks with clear diction & appropriate intonation
	Year 1 Term 2 5. Retell stories, ordering events using story language	Organises what to say
		Stores words effectively and chooses words with precision
		Focuses on the main points
	Year 1 Term 3 9. Interpret a text by reading aloud with some variety in pace and emphasis	Understands the basic vocabulary
		Understands basic grammar
		Speaks with appropriate intonation

Strategies, Activities and Resources	Language Area	Strategy Number	
• Special talk time		26	
• Conversational cue cards		23	
• Home–school link book		18	
• Feelings cue cards		28	
• Sentence building activities		20, 25	
• Sequencing activities		11	
• Use of modelling		3	
• Language Master		19	
• Vocabulary board		8	
• Avoid asking pupil to repeat		2	
• Sequencing activities		11	
• Model order of action matching order of mention		5	
• Systematic vocabulary teaching		15	
• Sorting and classifying activities		28, 29	
• Reinforce word meanings and definitions		2, 18	
• Mind mapping		36	
• Topic cue cards		37	
• Story planners		25	
• Word definition games		18	
• Sentence boxes		8	
• Phonological skills development		Select	

YEAR 1 SPEAKING

Key Stage 1 Strand One: Speaking

Broad Objectives *Programmes of Study*	Specific Objectives *Primary Strategy: Speaking, Listening and Learning*	Skills
SPEAKING Speaks clearly, fluently and confidently to different people	**Year 2 Term 1** 13. To speak with clarity and use intonation when reading and reciting texts	Speaks clearly
		Understands the text
		Is aware of rhythm in words and phrases
	Year 2 Term 2 17. Tell real and imagined stories using the conventions of familiar story language	Includes relevant detail
		Understands that stories have a beginning, middle and end
		Uses imagination
	Year 2 Term 3 21. Use language and gesture to support the use of models/diagrams/ displays when explaining	Ability to give instructions
		Uses appropriate gesture
		Ability to describe

Strategies, Activities and Resources	Language Area	Strategy Number
• Work on a variety of speech sound activities		Select
• Model sounds		31
• Work on sound discrimination		41, 42, 43
• Work on understanding at word and sentence level		Select
• Develop a sense of rhythm		33, 41
• Use clapping		25, 26
• Mind mapping		36
• Group speaking (for confidence)		7
• Remember what to say		10
• Provide a story framework		22, 25
• Playmobil stories		9
• Barrier games with instruction element		34
• Pair work, one able pupil talking, the language impaired pupil providing gesture		36
• Use a task management board		12
• Develop the use of descriptive language		31, 32, 33, 34

YEAR 2 SPEAKING

Key Stage 2 Strand One: Speaking

Broad Objectives *Programmes of Study*	Specific Objectives *Primary Strategy: Speaking, Listening and Learning*	Skills
SPEAKING Speak with confidence in a range of contexts, adapting speech for a range of purposes and audiences	**Year 3 Term 1** 25. Explain a process or present information, ensuring items are clearly sequenced, relevant details are included and accounts ended effectively	Understands the process
		Prioritises main points
		Sequences the process
		Is able to describe
		Can use notes/pictures to remember what to say
	Year 3 Term 2 29. Choose and prepare poems or stories for performance, identifying appropriate expression, tone, volume and use of voice and other sounds	Aware of a range of stories and poems
		Is confident to speak aloud
		Developing emotional literacy
		Aware of mood and atmosphere
	Year 3 Term 3 33. Sustain conversation, explaining or giving reasons for their views or choices	Stays on topic
		Takes turns in conversation
		Discusses cause and effect
		Remembers main points

Strategies, Activities and Resources	Language Area	Strategy Number
• Mind map key points		36
• Check understanding		3
• Teach vocabulary in meaningful situations		5, 6, 7, 8
• Topic cue cards		37
• Provide diagram of sequence		42
• Model skills through visual timetables		9
• Make order of action match order of mention		5
• Use of task management board		12
• Develop use of descriptive language		31, 32, 33, 34
• Provide talking frame		22
• Develop the use of complex grammatical skills		12–21
• Sentence boxes		8
• Group speaking		7
• Collective stories		20
• Feelings Cue Cards		28
• Role-play – How is he/she feeling?		30, 34
• Use instruments/film sound tracks for discussion		33
• Special Talk Time		26
• Play turn-taking activities		24
• Use social communication rules		22, 23
• 'Why? . . . because' LDA cards		Resource
• Provide talking frame		22

YEAR 3 SPEAKING

Key Stage 2 Strand One: Speaking

Broad Objectives *Programmes of Study*	Specific Objectives *Primary Strategy: Speaking, Listening and Learning*	Skills
SPEAKING Speak with confidence in a range of contexts, adapting speech for a range of purposes and audiences	**Year 4 Term 1** 37. Use and reflect on some ground rules for dialogue	Is aware that there are rules governing conversational skills
	Year 4 Term 2 41. Respond appropriately to the contributions of others in the light of alternative viewpoints	Has theory of mind
		Considers what others say
		Remembers what has been said
		Can disagree politely
	Year 4 Term 3 44. Tell stories using voice effectively	Speaks clearly
		Has basic grammar
		Understands what is being said
		Understands basic emotions
		Can 'role-play' a variety of characters/ moods etc.

Strategies, Activities and Resources	Language Area	Strategy Number
• Active listening		27
• Turn taking in conversation		22, 23, 24
• Social communication skills activities		Select
• Create a social story		27
• Assess using the Sally Anne/Smartie Test	Glossary	
• Social communication skills activities		Select
• 10-second Rule		3
• Cartoon strips		24
• Use a social story		27
• Work on a variety of speech sound activities		Select
• Modelling		3, 4
• Group speaking (for confidence)		7
• Key vocabulary understanding		Select
• Feelings cue cards		28
• Voice/emphasis activities		35
• Playmobil stories		9

YEAR 4 SPEAKING

Key Stage 2 Strand One: Speaking

Broad Objectives Programmes of Study	Specific Objectives Primary Strategy: Speaking, Listening and Learning	Skills
SPEAKING Speak with confidence in a range of contexts, adapting speech for a range of purposes and audiences	**Year 5 Term 1** 48. Tell a story using notes designed to cue techniques, such as repetition, recap and humour	Recognises the needs of the listener
		Is aware of different techniques to tell a story
		Is able to plan/follow a plan in a structured/ organised way
		Remembers what has to be said
	Year 5 Term 2 52. Use and explore different question types	Understands the difference between when, where, who, why and how
	Year 5 Term 3 55. Present a spoken argument, sequencing points logically, defending views with evidence and making use of persuasive language	Speaks clearly
		Understands the concept of the argument
		Sequences main points
		Remembers what has to be said

Strategies, Activities and Resources	Language Area	Strategy Number	
• Social communication skills activities		Select	
• Teach rehearsal techniques		6, 18	
• Develop a sense of humour		12	
• Talking frame		22	
• 10-second Rule		3	
• External memories		25	
• Question Cue Cards		Resource	
• Question/answer activities		43	
• 'What is it?' board		Resource	
• News time questions		13	
• Work on a variety of speech exercises		Select	
• 'How to be brilliant at' series		Resource	
• Key vocabulary development		Select	
• Flow diagrams		42	
• Prompt cards		22	
• Use a talking frame		22	

YEAR 5 SPEAKING

Key Stage 2 Strand One: Speaking

Broad Objectives *Programmes of Study*	Specific Objectives *Primary Strategy: Speaking, Listening and Learning*	Skills
SPEAKING Speak with confidence in a range of contexts, adapting speech for a range of purposes and audiences	**Year 6 Term 1** 58. Use a range of oral techniques to present persuasive argument	Has advanced vocabulary skills
		Is able to construct complex sentences in a logical sequence
		Is able to use conversational skills to discuss/debate/provide information
	Year 6 Term 2 62. Participate in whole-class debate using the conventions and language of debate, including standard English	Confident speaker
		Developing intermediate grammar skills
		Good word-finding skills
		Remembers what has to be said
		Good social skills
	Year 6 Term 3 65. Use techniques of dialogic talk to explore ideas, topics or issues	Listens to others in pairs, groups and whole class
		Understands another's point of view
		Remembers own view point
		Explains opinion effectively

Strategies, Activities and Resources	Language Area	Strategy Number
• Use mind mapping	BIG GROSS GIGANTIC ENORMOUS HUGE TALL	36
• Reinforce word meanings		2, 5, 17, 18
• Talking frames	99	22
• Role play	two faces	30, 34
• Develop miming skills		36
• Scaffold talking experience in a variety of situations	two faces	29, 34
• Cue in to useful phrases	99	26
• Learn key words prior to debate	BIG GROSS GIGANTIC ENORMOUS HUGE TALL	8
• External memory strategies	lightbulb	3, 25
• Social communication skills activities		Select
• Group rules	two faces	22
• Social communication skills activities		Select
• 10-second Rule	headphones	3
• Learn key words prior to discussion/debate	BIG GROSS GIGANTIC ENORMOUS HUGE TALL	8
• External memory strategies	lightbulb	3, 25
• Talking frame	99	22

YEAR 6 SPEAKING

Key Stage 1 Strand Two: Listening

Broad Objectives *Programmes of Study*	Specific Objectives *Primary Strategy: Speaking, Listening and Learning*	Skills
LISTENING Listen, understand and respond to others	**Year 1 Term 1** 2. Listen with sustained concentration	Motivated to listen
		Listens as a member of a class or group
		Listens actively
		Understands what is being said
	Year 1 Term 2 6. Listen and follow instructions accurately, asking for help and clarification if necessary	Listens actively
		Remembers what is being said
		Understands the words
		Knows when has not understood
	Year 1 Term 3 10. Listen to tapes or videos and express views about how a story or information has been presented	Understands and uses appropriate vocabulary
		Remembers information
		Identifies what has not been understood

Strategies, Activities and Resources	Language Area	Strategy Number
• Simplify language		1, 7
• Alert pupil by name/cue card		2
• Play listening games		14, 15
• Teach active listening		27
• Sound discrimination activities		22–24
• Check understanding		3
• Structure vocabulary		15
• Reinforce word meanings		2, 17, 18
• Teach active listening		27
• Use task management boards		12
• Classifying and sorting activities		28, 29
• Word definition games		17, 18
• Secure attention		2
• Teach how to seek clarification		28
• Visualising		19
• Listening skills extension activity		20
• Provide vocabulary board		38
• Create a story résumé board		47
• Use a comic strip		11
• Provide visual clues such as topic cue cards		15, 37
• Teach how to seek clarification		6
• Listen for specific information		16

YEAR 1 LISTENING

Key Stage 1 Strand Two: Listening

Broad Objectives *Programmes of Study*	Specific Objectives *Primary Strategy: Speaking, Listening and Learning*	Skills
LISTENING Listen, understand and respond to others	**Year 2 Term 1** 14. Listens to others in class, asks relevant questions and follows instructions	Developing social communication skills
		Understands what is being said
		Remembers what others have said
		Understands question words
	Year 2 Term 2 18. Responds to presentations by describing characters, repeating some highlights and commenting constructively	Knows a variety of adjectives
		Remembers significant features
		Expresses thoughts
	Year 2 Term 3 22. Listens to a talk by an adult, remembers some specific points and identifies what they have learned	Attends to adult and sustains listening
		Remembers some information
		Recognises and understands new knowledge/information

Strategies, Activities and Resources	Language Area	Strategy Number
• Teach social communication rules for whole class work		22, 23
• Vocabulary skills development		Select
• Use additional visual clues		7
• Develop working auditory memory		Select
• Chunk information		1
• Play barrier games		34
• Question word cue cards		Resource
• Word definition activities		18
• Use concrete examples		5
• Topic cue cards		37
• Use a story plan		25
• Role play activities		30, 34
• Secure pupil's attention		2
• Teach active listening		27
• Listen for specific sounds or words		17
• Mind-mapping		36
• Mind map before and after talk		36
• Teach vocabulary in meaningful situations		5, 6, 7, 8

YEAR 2 LISTENING

57

Key Stage 2 Strand Two: Listening

Broad Objectives *Programmes of Study*	Specific Objectives *Primary Strategy: Speaking, Listening and Learning*	Skills
LISTENING Listen, understand and respond appropriately to others	**Year 3 Term 1** 26. Follows up others' points and shows whether they agree or disagree in whole-class discussion	Listens to a range of voice types
		Takes turns in conversation
		Remembers key points
		Has own opinion
	Year 3 Term 2 30. Identifies the presentational features used to communicate the main points in a broadcast	Understands the key vocabulary
		Sustains visual concentration
		Identifies what presentational features are helpful/unhelpful
	Year 3 Term 3 34. Identifies key sections of an informative broadcast, noting how the language used signals changes or transitions in focus	Understands key vocabulary
		Conversational skills

Strategies, Activities and Resources	Language Area	Strategy Number	
• Work on sound discrimination		22	
• Teach active listening		27	
• Turn-taking activities		24	
• Play speaker, listener, observer		18	
• Use mind maps		36	
• Use prompt cards		37	
• Work on similarities and differences		4	
• For and against forms		48	
• Work on open and closed question techniques		43	
• Sorting and classification activities		28, 29	
• Reinforce word meanings		2, 17, 18	
• School routine cue cards to watch and listen		8	
• Use comic strips		11	
• Sorting activities based on presentational features		45	
• Sorting and classification activities		28, 29	
• Reinforce word meanings		2, 17, 18	
• Listening for specific information		16	
• Develop understanding of shifts in topic		3	

YEAR 3 LISTENING

Key Stage 2 Strand Two: Listening

Broad Objectives *Programmes of Study*	Specific Objectives *Primary Strategy: Speaking, Listening and Learning*	Skills
LISTENING Listen, understand and respond appropriately to others	**Year 4 Term 1** 38. Compare the different contributions of music, words and images in short extracts from TV programmes	Sustains visual and auditory concentration
		Can identify characteristics in music, words and images that help support understanding
	Year 4 Term 2 42. Listens to a speaker, makes notes on the talk and uses the notes as a basis for improvisation	Processes language
		Can précis main points
		Is able to listen and write simultaneously
		Wide vocabulary store
	Year 4 Term 3 45. Investigates how talk varies with age, familiarity, gender and purpose	Developing social communication skills
		Empathy towards others
		Wide experience of different social settings

Strategies, Activities and Resources	Language Area	Strategy Number
• Cue cards to watch and listen		27
• Use pop music		24
• Media lotto		32, 33
• Awareness of recorded sound		35
• Develop vocabulary to discuss presentation styles		45
• Visual cueing		7
• Secure pupil's attention		2
• Mind-mapping for note-taking		12
• Use of dictaphone		31
• Vocabulary skills development		Select
• Use group rules		22, 23
• Social communication skills activities		Select
• Assess using the Sally Anne/Smartie Test	Glossary	
• Visits to a range of settings		34

YEAR 4 LISTENING

61

Key Stage 2 Strand Two: Listening

Broad Objectives *Programmes of Study*	Specific Objectives *Primary Strategy: Speaking, Listening and Learning*	Skills
LISTENING Listen, understand and respond appropriately to others	**Year 5 Term 1** 49. Identifies some aspects of talk which vary between formal and informal occasions	Experience of formal/informal situations
	Year 5 Term 2 52. Identifies different question types and evaluates impact on audience	Is aware that different responses are elicited depending on the way questions are asked
	Year 5 Term 3 55. Analyses the use of persuasive language	Understands language to do with emotion
		Can empathise with others
		Identifies persuasive language in relation to advertising

Strategies, Activities and Resources	Language Area	Strategy Number	
• Work on the differences between how you talk/behave in different settings		29	
• Sorting, with pictures, formal/informal situations		34	
• Role playing formal/informal situations		30	
• Work on questioning techniques		43	
• News time questioning		13	
• Feelings cue cards		28	
• Role play		30	
• Use group rules		22, 23	
• Persuasive vocabulary development		46	

YEAR 5 LISTENING

Key Stage 2 Strand Two: Listening

Broad Objectives *Programmes of Study*	Specific Objectives *Primary Strategy: Speaking, Listening and Learning*	Skills
LISTENING Listen, understand and respond appropriately to others	**Year 6 Term 1** 59. Analyses and evaluates how speakers present points effectively through the use of language and gesture	Understands that information has been understood easily because speaker used effective communication skills
	Year 6 Term 2 62. Makes notes when listening for a sustained period and discusses how note-taking varies depending on context and purpose	Has good language processing skills
		Can use a variety of note-taking techniques
		Can select the most useful note-taking technique to meet the outcome required
	Year 6 Term 3 66. Listens for language variation in formal and informal contexts	Has good listening skills
		Is able to adjust language according to conversational partner and context, i.e. where communication is taking place

Strategies, Activities and Resources	Language Area	Strategy Number	
• Social communication skills small group work		29	
• Role-play		30, 34	
• Work on auditory skills		Select	
• Discuss the use of mind-mapping, cartoon strips, bullet points, key words and phrases		3, 12, 25	
• Use of dictaphone		31	
• Use a Language Master		Resource	
• Discuss the use of mind-mapping, cartoon strips, bullet points, key words and phrases		3, 12, 25	
• Use of dictaphone		31	
• Use a Language Master		37	
• Teach active listening		27	
• Social communication skills small group work		29	
• Role-play		30, 34	

YEAR 6 LISTENING

Performance Descriptions (P-levels) and Speaking and Listening Skills

The P-levels provide practitioners with attainment targets below Level 1.

P-Levels	Skills	Language Area
P4		
Repeat, copy and imitate between 10 and 50 single words, signs or phrases	Listens	
	Able to produce speech sounds	
Use single words, signs and symbols for familiar objects, to communicate about events and feelings	Can name familiar objects and has language for basic emotions	
	Uses language for social purposes	
Respond appropriately to simple requests that contain one key word, sign or symbol in familiar situations	Attends to, remembers and carries out simple, routine instructions containing one word, e.g. 'drink?'	
Demonstrate an understanding of at least 50 words, including the names of familiar objects	Developing some semantic knowledge	
P5		
Combines two key ideas or concepts	Developing the ability to construct simple phrases	

P-Levels	Skills	Language Area
P5		67
Combines single words, signs or symbols to communicate meaning to a range of listeners (e.g. 'Mummy gone'). Makes attempts to repair misunderstandings without changing the words used. Uses vocabulary of over 50 words.	Has basic social awareness	
	Knows that language helps to get needs met	
	Is extending vocabulary skills	
Follows requests and instructions containing two key words, signs or symbols	Listens and processes at a two-word level	
Responds appropriately to questions about familiar or immediate events or experiences	Understands simple question words, i.e. 'what?' or 'where?'	
P6		
Initiates and maintains short conversations using preferred method of communication	Is developing social communication skills	
Ask simple questions to obtain information, e.g. 'What is your name?'	Is aware and interested in other people and the environment	
Uses prepositions, such as 'in' or 'on' and pronouns, such as 'my' or 'it' correctly	Is developing understanding of abstract concepts and grammatical skills	
Follows requests and instructions with three key words, signs or symbols and responds to others in group situations, e.g. taking turns appropriately	Understands language that contains nouns, verbs and adjectives	
	Developing understanding of simple grammar	
	Is developing social skills	

67

P-Levels	Skills	Language Area
P7		
Uses phrases with up to three key words, signs or symbols to communicate simple ideas, events or stories to others	Language includes nouns, verbs and adjectives	
	Is developing basic grammar	
	Is motivated to communicate	
Communicates ideas about present, past and future events and experiences, using simple phrases and statements	Is motivated to communicate simple ideas	
	Has basic time concepts	
	Has basic grammar	
Uses regular plurals correctly and the conjunction 'and' to link ideas or add new information beyond what is asked	Has understanding of concept of more than one and grammatical knowledge	
Listens, attends to and follow stories for short stretches of time	Developing attention control Developing active listening	
	Understands the meaning of simple vocabulary	
	Developing working auditory memory	
Follows requests and instructions with four key words, signs or symbols	Has basic attention control	
	Is able to process instructions with adjectives, verbs and nouns	

68

P-Levels	Skills	Language Area
P7		69
Contributes appropriately one-to-one and in small group discussions and role-play	Developing turn-taking skills	
	Stays on topic	
	Has empathy towards others	
	Is developing imaginative play	
Attends to, and responds to, questions from adults and peers about experiences, events and stories	Ability to retain some basic information	
	Developing word-finding skills	
	Developing basic expressive grammar	
P8		
Uses an extensive vocabulary to convey meaning to the listener, using possessives and conjunctions	Developing vocabulary skills	
	Is developing grammatical knowledge	
Link up to four key words, signs or symbols to communicate about their own experiences or to tell familiar stories	Has basic word finding skills	
	Has basic expressive grammar	
	Can remember familiar information	
Takes part in role-play with confidence	Has empathy towards others	
	Understand that others may think differently	

Attainment Targets and Speaking and Listening Skills

Level 1 A.T.1

Pupils should be competent in the following skills to reach Level 1.

For ideas to develop these skills refer to the corresponding section in Chapter 5.

Statement / Order	Skills	Language Area
Able to talk about matters of immediate interest	Can name objects	
	Has basic grammar	
	Can stay on target Can express feelings	
Listens to others and usually responds appropriately	Ability to take turns	
	Has an interest in and a sympathy towards other people	
	Is beginning to understand social rules	
	Interprets signals, gestures and facial expression	
	Has basic grammatical understanding	
Speaks audibly	Articulation does not impede communication	
Extends ideas or accounts by providing some detail	Vocabulary includes some prepositions, adjectives, adverbs	
	Has basic expressive grammar	
	Ability to sequence ideas and events pictorially	
	Understands cause and effect Ability to stay on target	

Level 2 A.T.2

Pupils should be competent in the following skills to reach Level 2.

For ideas to develop these skills refer to the corresponding section in Chapter 5.

Statement / Order	Skills	Language Area
Shows confidence in talking and listening on topics that interest him/her	Developing grammatical expression	
	Articulation does not impede communication	
	Good attention control	
	Ability to understand more than basic grammar	
Awareness of the needs of the listeners by including relevant detail	Awareness of shared knowledge Ability to stay on target	
	Good use of vocabulary	
Developing and explaining ideas, speaking clearly and using growing vocabulary	Ability to sequence ideas and events Knowledge of a range of concepts	
	Good understanding of cause and effect	
	Clear articulation	
	Vocabulary includes use of prepositions, adjectives and adverbs	
	Grammar includes some use of past and future tense	

Level 2 A.T.2 (cont'd)

Statement / Order	Skills	Language Area
Listening carefully and responding with increasing appropriateness to what others have to say	Ability to listen actively, taking responsibility for not understanding	
	Developing organisational skills	
	Understands rules in simple games	
	Good comprehension	
	Answers questions without mixing 'what', 'when' and 'where'	
Becoming aware of situations where more formal vocabulary and tone of voice are used	Understands social rules	
	Interprets signals, gestures, facial expression, moods and situations reasonably accurately	

Level 3 A.T.1

Pupils should be competent in the following skills to reach Level 3.

For ideas to develop these skills refer to the corresponding section in Chapter 5.

Statement / Order	Skills	Language Area
Can talk and listen confidently in different contexts, exploring and communicating ideas	Can focus attention while distractions are present	
	Questions facts	
	Is developing a sense of humour – understands and tells basic jokes	
	Understands and applies different social rules	
	Ability to vary pitch and speed of voice	
Understands main points in a discussion	Can maintain attention when focus changes	
	Can classify and sort information Has good short-term memory	
	Has sound reasoning skills	
Can demonstrate careful listening through relevant comments and questions	Takes responsibility for not understanding	
	Is able to organise thoughts Good short-term memory	
	Understand complex grammar	
	Ability to learn new vocabulary	

Level 3 A.T.1 (cont'd)

Statement / Order	Skills	Language Area
Begins to adapt what is said to the needs of the listener, varying the use of vocabulary and level of detail	Ability to predict	
	Ability to modify behaviour	
	Ability to be selective	
Awareness of standard English and when to use it	Can adjust to the demands of social communication	

Level 4 A.T.1

Pupils should be competent in the following skills to reach Level 4.

For ideas to develop these skills refer to the corresponding section in Chapter 5.

Statement / Order	Skills	Language Area
Pupil talks and listens with confidence in an increasing range of contexts, including some that are of a formal nature	Is confident in the skills acquired at Level 3	
Talk is adapted to the purpose: developing ideas thoughtfully, describing events and conveying his/her opinion clearly	Sophisticated awareness of social rules	
	Ability to use language to conceptualise	
	Good sequencing skills	
	Good use of adverbs and adjectives	
	Is developing independent thinking	
In discussion, listens carefully, making contributions and asking questions that are responsive to others' ideas and views	Ability to receive and process auditory information	
	Good active-listening skills	
	Interested in and aware of other people	
Some of the features of standard English are used appropriately in formal situations	Complicated grammatical sentence structure is understood and used	

Level 5 A.T.1

Pupils should be competent in the following skills to reach Level 5.

For ideas to develop these skills refer to the corresponding section in Chapter 5.

Statement / Order	Skills	Language Area
Talks and listens confidently in a wide range of different contexts, exploring and communicating ideas	Understands and uses social rules appropriately with a range of people and settings	
	Seeks clarification	
	Can understand and hold on to more than one concept or key point	
Engages the interest of the listener as they begin to vary their expression and vocabulary	Uses appropriate tone, pitch, volume and pace when speaking	
	Has a wide vocabulary	
In discussion, they pay close attention to what others say, ask questions to develop ideas, make contributions that take account of others' views	Has good active listening skills	
	Seeks clarification	
	Empathises with others' points of view	
Begins to use standard English in formal situations	Is aware that some situations require a more formal use of language without being told	

Level 6 A.T.1

Pupils should be competent in the following skills to reach Level 6.

For ideas to develop these skills refer to the corresponding section in Chapter 5.

Statement / Order	Skills	Language Area
Talk to the demands of different contexts with increasing confidence	Is confident in the skills acquired at Level 5	
Talk engages the interest of the listener through the variety of its vocabulary and expression	Has a wide range of concrete, abstract and subject specific vocabulary	
	Uses appropriate intonation confidently	
In discussion, pupils take an active part, showing understanding of ideas and a sensitivity to others	Is confident in the skills acquired at Level 5	
Fluent in their use of standard English in formal situations	Is confident in the skills acquired at Level 5	

5 | Strategies for Use across the Curriculum

This chapter provides practitioners with a wealth of strategy and activity ideas to support pupils with language and communication difficulties across all areas of the curriculum.

It is divided into the six areas of language identified in Chapter 2. Each section is colour- and symbol-coded and contains the observed behaviours for difficulties in each area of language, whole class strategies and small group activities.

Language development should not be seen as separate from the delivery of the National Curriculum. Strategy ideas can be adapted to make all language learning opportunities curriculum friendly.

When choosing strategies it is important to consider the whole context rather than focusing on specific individual needs alone. Consider how strategies and resources can be used in whole class and small group work. Working in this way will be of benefit to other pupils in the classroom and will help to promote the development of speaking and listening skills. Therefore, many of the ideas suggested in this chapter are either whole class or small group based.

Attention and Listening

Observed Behaviours:

- Difficulties sitting still during whole-class teaching
- Focuses attention very briefly
- Does not respond when asking the whole class to listen
- Difficulties staying on task
- Instructions need to be simplified in order to be understood
- Does not comply with instructions
- Relies on peers and copies their actions
- Is used to not understanding so does not question
- Gets lost within an activity

Communication Techniques for Practitioners

1 Give clear, short instructions and 'chunk' information. Be aware of how many information – carrying words are being used; e.g. 'Get your **number book** from your **drawer**; on a **clean page, write** the **date** and **draw** a **square'** contains at least nine information-carrying words, too many for a pupil with difficulties in understanding instructions.

2 Secure the pupil's attention before giving an instruction, for instance by calling his/her name.

3 Use the '10-second Rule' – once you have given an instruction, allow the pupil ten seconds to respond. During this time, consider the instruction: Too many words? Was the vocabulary too difficult to understand? If the pupil does not respond after 10 seconds, either rephrase the instruction or, if the right level of language was used the first time, simply repeat the instruction again.

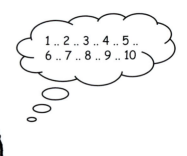

4 Use positive statements about what the pupil should do, e.g. say 'walk' instead of 'don't run'.

5   Give instructions in the same order as the action required, e.g. 'It's PE then break time', rather than 'before break time it's PE'.

6   Encourage the use of rehearsal and check understanding by asking open-ended questions after information has been given, e.g. 'Which book do you have to use?'; 'What do you have to do?'.

General Strategies and Activities

7   Use visual cues, gestures and/or signing to accompany verbal instructions or information, e.g. have pictures illustrating topic work handy to accompany new vocabulary or concepts. Incorporate some sign language to give another clue when giving instructions.

8   Use school routine cue cards to support pupils' understanding of general classroom instructions, for instance 'time to sit on the carpet', 'playtime next'. Simply show the picture at the same time as giving the instruction.

9   Introduce a visual timetable to help pupils to understand what will be happening during the school day, to support sequencing and recall skills and to teach understanding of specific time concepts.

10 Give pupils a verbal message to give to another member of staff or class. The message should require an answer so that it is clear that the instruction was delivered correctly. Sending the pupil on an errand to get something from a cupboard etc. would also give the child experience in grammatical understanding.

11 Support listening and processing of new information by providing a 'comic strip' series of pictures illustrating the main points:

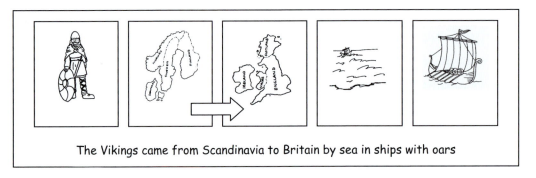

The Vikings came from Scandinavia to Britain by sea in ships with oars

12 Support the pupil's ability to listen to and understand instructions by using task management boards that provide pictorial support for the stages within a single activity:

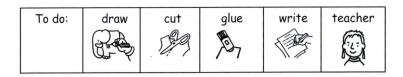

'Draw the picture, cut it out, stick it on some card, write your name on the back and then go to the teacher'.

13 Sit pupils in a circle: ask each pupil in turn to tell the rest of the class something about themselves. When everyone has had a go, ask questions like, 'What did Andrew say?' or 'Who has a pet snake?'. Adapt this for news time. Direct each pupil to give one item of news, then ask the rest of the class to retell someone else's news, e.g. 'Cathy said that she went to her Nan's'.

14 Play 'Chinese Whispers' while lining up for PE, playtime, etc. Begin with very simple, short sentences using familiar vocabulary.

15 Play 'Simon Says' while lining up or warming up.

16 Ask pupils to listen out for specific information before telling a story or listening to a TV programme. For example, 'I want you to listen for the types of food the Saxons eat and the games the children liked playing', etc. Different information could be listened for by different pupils, so varying the level of difficulty.

17 Read a passage / story / poem. Ask pupils to clap when they hear a particular word or sound, e.g. 'Roman' or 'sh'.

18 Play 'Speaker, Listener, Observer'. The speaker tells a group about something, the listener retells the incident, then the observer comments on how much information the listener remembered. At first it is best if the speaker is an adult who keeps the 'story' very simple.

19 Ask pupils to visualise themselves doing what they have been asked to do, as they are being told. This could be supported by digital photographs.

20 Use photographs or objects to develop the ability to process instructions. Select a group of pictures that belong together, e.g. children's clothes, then suggest an activity, such as going to the beach for the day. Say to the pupil, 'You are going to the beach for the day. It's hot so you will need to take your swimming things, a hat, an anorak and your flip-flops'. The pupil selects these objects. Gradually increase the number you ask for and increase the difficulty of processing by including objects of, say, different colours and asking for a particular one. This strategy is easily adapted for use within the curriculum, e.g. 'Go to the hall and set out the following equipment, six hoops, six balls, six bean bags and six ropes'. Give the pupil(s) a photograph of how it should look. Next time let them look at the photograph, but not take it with them. Finally, expect them to do it without a visual cue.

21 Start the lesson with a short focusing activity, e.g. if it's numeracy count to 20 in twos. If it's art and craft hold up items of equipment and ask the class to mime the function, e.g. scissors – cutting action.

22 Play auditory discrimination games such as 'Sound Lotto' (LDA) or tape the voices of the children in the group. Play back the tape and point to the correct child as their voice, giggle etc. is heard. Do the same with members of staff, calling out their name or pointing to their photograph. Familiar sounds around the school can also be recorded and linked to

83

pictures either cut from catalogues or taken with a digital camera, e.g. guillotine, fire alarm, sports whistle etc.

23 Play 'Listen to the Silence': sit very quietly whispering the names of the things that can be heard.

24 Play an unfamiliar pop song, then ask pupils what instruments they could hear or what lyrics they remembered.

25 Play 'Join in Clap': one person claps a simple rhythm and each pupil joins in, in turn, until everyone is clapping the same rhythm.

26 Play 'Copy Clap': as above but pupils take it in turns so that they have to remember the rhythm.

Specific Strategies

27 Teach 'active listening' by showing pupils that in order to listen effectively they must sit still, look at the speaker and think about what is being said (Johnson 2001). Use picture cue cards to support pupils' understanding of each skill.

28 Develop children's ability to take responsibility for not understanding: encourage them to have the confidence to tell you if they a) couldn't hear; b) didn't understand the words you used; c) that you were speaking too quickly, etc.

29 Introduce group rules during small group work, identifying key social communication skills to be developed. For instance, good listening, waiting for a turn to speak and looking at the speaker.

30 Develop the use of mind-mapping (Buzan 2003) to assist note-taking.

31 Use a dictaphone for recording vital information to play back repeatedly or for recording pupils' ideas so they will not be forgotten.

32 Play Sound Lotto using signature tunes of familiar TV programmes.

33 Play Sound Lotto using background music/voices for different types of programmes, i.e. horror, cartoon, sports, comedy etc.

34 Play barrier games: put a screen between two pupils and introduce activities that require giving and receiving instructions. Use worksheets that contain rows of different animals, shapes, etc. (visual discrimination sheets are good, patterns can be added to make them all different). Each pupil has a blank sheet and an identical set of coloured pencils; each pupil takes it in turn to give an instruction like. 'Colour the second fish blue' or 'Colour the spotted bird red', etc. Both pupils then carry out the instruction. The sheets are compared at the end. This can also be done using an identical set of lego pieces ('Put four white bricks on the black base' etc.), drawing pictures or making play-dough models. Make up picture sheets of current topic vocabulary such as 'Shapes', 'Invaders and Settlers', 'Forces and Motion' etc.

35 Develop an awareness of how voices/sounds affect what is heard by providing recorded examples and a recording sheet.

	Good	Bad	Why
Voice 1			
Voice 2			
Voice 3			
Voice 4			
Music 1			
Music 2			
Music 3			
Music 4			
Sound effect 1			
Sound effect 2			
Sound effect 3			
Sound effect 4			

36 Use peer support through pair work: able pupil presents story or information to an audience while his/her partner (pupil with language difficulties) provides gesture/picture cue cards.

37 Use a Language Master (Drake Educational) to record key instructions.

Commercially Available Material

- Active Listening cue cards – Language for Learning
- Seeking Clarification cue cards – Language for Learning
- Visual Timetable picture packs – Language for Learning
- Task Management boards – Language for Learning
- Language Master – Drake Educational
- Sound Lotto – LDA
- Sound Stories – LDA
- Look Hear! – LDA
- Listen, Think & Do – LDA
- Talking Traffic – LDA
- Animal Soundtracks – Living and Learning
- Listening Skills – Questions Publications
- Early Listening Skills – Winslow
- Developing Alert Listening Skills – Winslow
- Good Listening and Good Talking posters – TaskMaster
- The Language Gap – AMS Educational
- Find Your Fish – Philip & Tacey

Understanding the Meaning of Words

Observed Behaviours:

- Has difficulty learning new vocabulary
- Finds it difficult to understand language – both at a single word and sentence level
- Is unable to recall known words
- Word finding difficulties, i.e. uses 'yacht' instead of 'boat'; 'clock' instead of 'watch'
- Difficulties understanding and retaining abstract concepts
- Experiences difficulties defining words
- Difficulties processing language at a sentence level
- Difficulties reading for meaning
- Is used to not understanding so may not question

General Principles for Developing Semantic Skills at a Single Word Level

1 Adopt a systematic approach to teaching new vocabulary – choose both concrete and abstract concepts related to topic vocabulary and prioritise the vocabulary for pupils to understand/use.

2 Reinforce the meaning of the word, not just the label/name; for example, 'It's a plant, you find it in the garden and it grows'.

3 Check understanding by asking open-ended questions after information has been given, e.g. 'Which book do you have to use?'

4 Develop awareness of 'same' and 'different'. Identify the differences between words to help pupils to develop new word concepts by sorting and categorising.

5 Teach new vocabulary in meaningful learning situations, using real objects and tapping into visual, auditory and kinaesthetic learning styles.

6 Do not assume that a pupil will generalise the use of vocabulary from one context to another – provide visual clues to help pupils to do this.

7 Teach words in sentences rather than in isolation, e.g. 'We heat the room with a ....' (radiator). 'We go out to play when we hear the ....' (bell)'. Egyptians lived on the banks of the ....' (Nile). Where possible cue in with a picture.

8 If possible, provide pre-teaching opportunities. Use topic books suitable for younger pupils so that information can be 'scaffolded' from simple to more difficult. Discuss word meanings using pictures, then draw from memory to reinforce language concepts; for example, within the topic of 'Humans and other animals' – draw a spider's eight legs, counting as they are drawn, and attach a web. Then draw a ladybird counting its legs as they are drawn. Identify the differences.

Communication Techniques for Practitioners

9 Reinforce vocabulary by giving the pupil experience of target words in as many different contexts and with as many different people as possible. Link new vocabulary to concrete objects, use in role-play situations and illustrate with pictures/symbols.

10 Reduce anxiety by not insisting on the correct word; be accepting of a description or a similar word, but use the correct word in your reply, e.g. 'It's in the – you know, the thing we keep the balls and the skipping ropes in.' Yes that's right; it's in the PE shed.'

11 Use visuals and sequencing to help pupils to remember a word by cueing-in with a phrase made up of shorter words, e.g. 'It's water in a can – it's a ....' (watering can). 'There's air round a plane – it's an ....' (aeroplane). 'The book's in a case – it's a ....' (bookcase). 'It's what you daub on the wall – ....' (wattle and daub). Pictures may also help.

12 Some pupils may find it helpful if you cue them in with the first initial sound, then first syllable, etc., e.g. 'py........ra........mid', etc. However, others may find this a distraction.

13 Some pupils need time to recall the appropriate word – it may be helpful to move on to the next question with another pupil, and ask the first pupil to let you know when he/she has remembered.

General Strategies

14 Have a list of the vocabulary to be learnt displayed in the classroom, e.g. 'The five words for this week are . . .', so that it is available to anyone working in the classroom.

15 Plan vocabulary and prioritise key vocabulary for pupils to learn. Find objects and pictures to support key vocabulary throughout topic work. For example:

Nouns	Functions	Categories	Attributes	Concepts
metal	touch	materials	hard	same
plastic	feel	natural	soft	different
wood	cut	man-made	rough	
paper	squeeze		smooth	
clay	bend			

16 Provide lists of target vocabulary for parents with some ideas to help reinforce the meaning of words across different contexts at home. Plan well in advance of topic work.

17 Use visual support to demonstrate how words are linked, for instance as a simple word web.

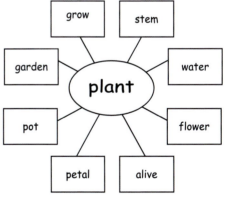

18 Word definition: Develop word definition skills by asking questions related to the meaning of a word; for instance, 'What do you do with?'; 'Where do you find it?'; 'What does it look like?' Use visual clues to support this and record the information for future reference on a simple word web.

19 Play barrier games – put a screen between two pupils and introduce activities that require giving and receiving instructions. Use worksheets that contain rows of different animals, shapes, etc. (visual discrimination sheets are good, patterns can be added to make them all different). Each pupil has a blank sheet and an identical set of coloured pencils. Each pupil takes it in turn to give an instruction like 'Colour the second fish blue' or 'Colour the spotted bird red', etc. Both pupils then carry out the instruction. The sheets are compared at the end. This can also be done using an identical set of lego pieces. ('Put four white bricks on the black base', etc.), drawing pictures or making play-dough models. Make up picture sheets of current topic vocabulary such as 'Shapes', 'Invaders and Settlers', 'Forces and Motion', etc.

20 Select pupils for different activities by description, e.g. 'If you have only sisters, go to the printing table', or, 'All pupils with blonde hair go to the model-making table, except those with brown eyes'. The level of difficulty will be determined by the pupils you are targeting for this area of concern.

21 Ask pupils to listen out for pre-specified information when verbal information is being given, for instance for a specific name, colour, verb, preposition, time or emotion. Start by reading a familiar story and asking pupils to put their hands up when they hear, for example, a boy's name or a word to do with time (before, after). Gradually increase the complexity of the story and ask for a reaction to more than one word.

Specific Strategies, Games and Activities

22 Play 'Listen and Guess': working with a small group or one-to-one, a set of objects, related to a current topic, is put in front of the pupils, the adult describes one of the objects, the pupil(s) guesses which object it is.

23 Play the game 'Fruit Salad': a group of related words is chosen, for example 'fruit'. The group of pupils sit in a circle and each one has to run round the circle calling out another fruit before sitting down. At any time the pupil whose go it is can call out the collective name for the group and everyone jumps up and runs round.

24 Play 'Pass the Parcel': either put objects or pictures of the vocabulary you are reinforcing between the layers of paper. When the music stops the player with the object/picture has to name it and say one thing about it. If the information is correct the object/picture is 'won'. The winner is the one who has the most objects/pictures at the end.

25 Play 'I went to market and I bought . . .'. Supply pictures of items pupils would not necessary think of to create the opportunity to extend their vocabulary.

26 Play 'Snap' and 'Pelmanism', matching words and word definitions with pictures.

27 Play 'I-Spy' using a description instead of a letter name, e.g. 'I spy with my little eye something that is round and shiny'.

28 Sorting and Classifying: provide opportunities to explore the meaning of words and the links between words through sorting and classification activities. Use as many different objects, pictures and ways of sorting as possible. Start with just two classifications, i.e. square and not square. Gradually increase the classifications up to four, i.e. squares, rectangles, circles, triangles.

29 Sort abstract words by linking them to concrete words; for example, lay out large pictures of a house, a person, a book, a flower and a dog. Link the following words to one or more of the pictures: solid, happy, beautiful, healthy, tall, delicate, hungry, grand, blue, heavy, homely, nervous, scary. This can be adapted for use during any topic work by selecting one to four concrete words and a group of abstract words from the key vocabulary plan.

30 Matching: cut pictures of the vocabulary you are teaching in half and arrange all the halves on the table, ask pupils to take it in turns to match and name. Start with objects that are dissimilar and gradually introduce ones that are more difficult to sort from each other.

31 Describing: once pupils understand the function and location of objects, teach them how to describe. To begin with, practise using two elements only: size and colour; for example, 'It's big and blue.' Gradually add words linked to the senses: 'What does it look like?', 'What does it feel like?'

'What does it sound like?', 'Does it have a taste?', 'Does it have a smell?'. Cue cards could be used with pictures drawn for size, colour, shape, texture, sound, taste and smell:

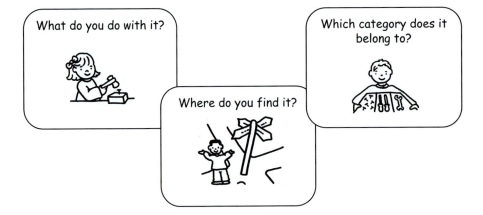

32 Describing: make cue cards as described above; give one to each pupil; pass an object round; each pupil has to say the right word to fit the cue card and the object, e.g. object: an orange – the pupil with the 'taste' cue card says 'sweet'; the pupil with the 'colour' cue card says 'orange', and so on. Gradually increase expectation so that the cue card word and the description is included and the pupil is repeating what has been said before, for example, 'It tastes sweet, it smells nice, it's orange-coloured and it feels bumpy'.

33 Describing: pupils take it in turns to practise describing people, objects and pictures to blindfolded pupils. Always have a cue card or object in front of the describer to help with the description, making sure that the pupils guessing have had a chance to look at the possibilities beforehand. It will also help if the description is discussed in relation to the object afterwards.

34 Describing: pass a simple, everyday object around a circle; each pupil adds a word to describe it, says what it could be used for, or thinks of other objects that go with it. This activity will work better if ideas for words are discussed first.

35 Miming: using a pile of action cards turned face down, pupils take it turns to pick up a card and mime the action; the rest try to guess what it is.

36 Mind-mapping: use mind-maps to provide visual semantic links between words. Arrange topic displays as a mind map. Provide simple mind-maps of

each curriculum topic and teach pupils to record their own work in mind-map form. Use mind-mapping to gather information about what pupils know before introducing new topic. Mind-map again once the topic is completed and compare the difference with pupils.

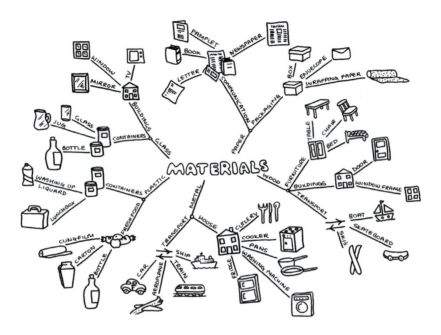

37 Use topic cue cards to provide visual reinforcement. Show pictures illustrating key vocabulary as new words are introduced. Continue to refer to these to reinforce meaning throughout the topic.

38 Provide vocabulary picture boards for individuals or groups to reinforce vocabulary and to support pupils' classification skills.

39 Use dictionaries organised by meaning rather than by initial sound. When pupils request a spelling, rather than asking for the initial sound, ask them to find the category or group of words that the word belongs to.

40 Use a Language Master (Drake Educational) to develop a talking glossary. Select the key vocabulary from the current topic; find a picture to represent each word and stick to a Language Master card. Record the word on the pupil track and a simple word definition on the teacher track. When pupils are unsure of a word, they can access the talking glossary.

41 Word association: play games with words, for example:

'Table and ....' (chair).

'Cup and ....' (saucer).

'Salt and ....' (pepper).

'Night and ....' (day).

Use pictures of the words to create a matching game.

42 Provide flow diagrams to support sequencing skills, e.g. of a seed growing into a plant.

43 Work on open and closed questioning techniques: do a survey using open and closed questions and compare the information gained from both.

44 Sort and classify types of television programmes – cartoons, news, soaps and documentaries. Cut up an evening's viewing from a television guide and sort into separate categories. Start with children's television programmes.

45 To learn vocabulary needed to talk about presentational styles; discuss the features in a television broadcast that help pupils to learn new material most effectively. Make cards with a picture to represent each feature, i.e. music, cartoon, graphics, charts, presenter, interviewer, stills and animation. Sort into helpful/not helpful.

46 Match 'selling slogans' to different types of shops/products, e.g. Fresh Fish, Juicy Fruits, Mouth-watering Melons, Crunchy Crisps, Glossy healthy hair, etc.

47 Make a story résumé book with a short entry for each book saying what the story is about and whether or not it was enjoyed. This is useful to build up a bank of vocabulary for discussions about the stories.

48 Work on understanding the concepts of arguments by providing a range of 'for' and 'against' recording forms.

Commercially Available Material

- Word Association Cue Cards – Language for Learning
- 'What is it?' boards and posters – Language for Learning
- Question Cue cards – Language for Learning
- Maths Concept Wheel – Language for Learning
- Photo cards – LDA
- Talking Traffic – LDA
- Colour cards – Winslow
- Combimage – Winslow
- Silly Bulls – Philip & Tacey
- Connexions – Philip & Tacey
- Where do I belong? – Philip & Tacey
- The If Game – Philip & Tacey
- Language Master – Drake Educational Associates
- The Language Gap – AMS Educational
- Homonyms/Synonyms – Smartkids
- Kidspiration – SEMERC
- 'How to be Brilliant at' series – Brilliant Publications
- Compound Word Chains – LDA
- Fun Decks – TaskMaster

Structure and Rules: Syntax

Observed Behaviours:

- Needs language simplified for complete understanding
- Misunderstands instructions or questions that contain negatives, pronouns, plurals and tenses
- Difficulties constructing sentences
- Uses immature sentence construction
- Uses telegrammatic sentences
- Gets words in the wrong order
- Uses the wrong word endings

General Principles

1   Introduce visual support to help pupils understand which elements are needed within a sentence.

2   Be aware that understanding of grammatical expression is closely linked with the ability to remember what has been said. Work on increasing the pupils' ability to understand using concrete objects. Make sure that they have a chance to familiarise themselves with the objects being used, so that an immediate link is made with the object and the instruction.

Communication Techniques for Practitioners

3   Avoid correcting pupils' poor grammar; rather use the correct form when replying, e.g. 'Him gived me is sweet', 'He gave you his sweet'.

4   When working on increasing the level of grammatical difficulty with the pupil, stress the key words but retain normal speech intonation.

General Strategies

5   Work on tense in relation to time using hand gestures. Place your left hand in front of you to indicate now/present, move it to your left hand side to indicate before/past, and move it to the right to indicate after/future, etc. Make sure the pupil you are working with is sitting beside, not opposite, you.

6   Puppets are always good to encourage shy pupils to talk and provide visual support. Start off with a simple dialogue between the adult and the puppet, gradually extending this to a dialogue between the adult's puppet and the pupil's puppet, and then on to a group of pupils with puppets.

7   Use stories or poems that have a lot of repetitive dialogue for class choral speaking, e.g. 'The Gingerbread Man'. Pupils all chant, 'Run, run as fast as you can, you can't catch me I'm the Gingerbread Man'. Adapt this kind of refrain to change the tense, e.g. 'He ran and ran as fast as a van but he couldn't catch the Gingerbread Man'.

8   Have a set of boxes available in the classroom labelled with basic elements of a sentence, for instance people, actions, objects, places, adjectives. Collect pictures to go in each box or use Combimage pictures (Winslow). Describe pictures or events by choosing a picture from a selection of the boxes, for instance a person, action and object and organise the pictures to make a sentence.

Specific Strategies

9   Use *Playmobil* figures to act out simple stories, rather like children do while play acting with dolls. As each 'person' in the story talks or does something, move the appropriate *Playmobil* piece.

10 Work on pronouns by making two circles of card, one with a picture of a boy and one with a girl. Then make a selection of playing cards each with a picture of either boy or a girl performing an action. Encourage the pupil(s) to put the playing card in the correct circle, saying, 'She's sleeping', or 'He's swimming', etc. Pictures for this game are produced by Black Sheep Press.

11 Use sequencing picture stories such as Fold-A-Book (Winslow) to develop syntax beyond a single sentence level.

12 Leave the person standing: play a game where the class stands up, the teacher or a pupil describes a member of the class, and after each sentence children sit down if that description does not fit them, e.g. 'It's a girl' (all the boys sit down), etc. Introduce prepositions, pronouns and complicated grammar as the children get used to the game.

13 Play 'Reporters'. Sit pupils in a circle; the first pupil whispers something that he/she has done that day to the pupil on his/her left; that pupil then reports what the first pupil had done to the rest of the class, using the past tense. Model the reply, e.g. 'Mary said that today she had '………………'.

14 With the class sitting in a circle take it in turns to practise 'Why? – Because' sentences. Have a series of action pictures such as a boy running, a dog wagging his tail, a slave dragging a stone up a wooden ramp, etc. Ask questions such as, 'Why is the boy running?'. Stress that the answer must start with, 'Because ………………'.

15 Ask each pupil to say something about him/herself in turn. The pupil to his/her left then repeats what he/she said using the correct pronoun. For example, first pupil: 'My hair is black'. Next pupil: 'Her hair is black'. Then that pupil says something about him/herself, etc.

16 Organise pupils into groups of two and three. While the class is sitting in a circle, ask them to mime something together, e.g. building a wall, singing in the choir, etc. The rest of the class guesses by saying, 'They're building a wall', etc.. If the guess is incorrect the miming group have to say, 'No, we were ………………'.

17 To develop grammatical skills, play 'Simon Says' using fairly complicated grammar, e.g. 'Before you touch your head, cough', or 'If there's a girl in the class called Anne, jump', etc.

18 A useful way of practising prepositions, nouns, tenses and verbs is to use a Language Master with a set of pre-recorded cards asking the child questions about either individual pictures stuck on Language Master cards, or one large picture. Questions could include, 'Where is the car?', 'What is the boy doing?', 'What is walking along the roof?', etc. The pupil can record the answers on the pupil track of the appropriate card.

19 Also using the Language Master, put speech bubbles on funny pictures and ask the pupil to record what the man is saying, etc.

20 Play 'Collective Stories': the adult starts a story finishing in mid-sentence, the next child continues, and so on around the group back to the adult who finishes it off. Start by retelling a familiar story or making one up about people or an event known to all the children.

21 Play 'Pelmanism' to encourage the use of the plural form: make a set of matching pairs of cards; spread face down on the table; players take it in turns to turn over two cards. If a matching pair is not turned over the pupil says, 'There's one dog and one cat'; however, if a matching pair is turned over the player has to say, 'There are two dogs'. The winner is the player with the most pairs.

22 Make Talking Frames, rather like writing frames to support pupils when they have to tell the class a story or explain how something has been made/works. Do not forget to include the beginning, middle and end. Consider the 'How To Be Brilliant At' recording series (Brilliant Publications).

23 Play 'Snap', 'Pelmanism' and sort formal/informal sentences, e.g. 'Hello Catherine' versus 'Hiya Cath'.

24 Have a photograph card of a well-known TV news reporter and a photo card of two friends talking. Match a range of formal and informal sentences about news items to either the friends or the TV newsreader.

25 Use a variety of story plans to support both sentence construction skills and the development of early narrative skills. Include beginning, middle, end, key questions (who?, when?, where?, what?) and character's feelings.

26 Work on key phrases to help express opinions, e.g.:

I like .... because ....

I don't like .... because ....

I think ...., but on the other hand ....

Commercially Available Material

- Brickworks – LDA
- Talespin – LDA
- 'What's wrong?' – LDA
- 'Why? ... because? – LDA
- Action Lotto – LDA
- Combimage – LDA
- BROGY – TaskMaster
- Grammar Game Boards – TaskMaster
- Yestersdays Verbs – TaskMaster
- Reception Narrative Pack – Black Sheep Press
- Pronouns – Black Sheep Press
- Fold a Book – Winslow
- Story cards – Winslow
- Language Steps – STASS
- Story Sixes – Philip & Tacey
- Writing with Symbols 2000 – Widgit Software
- Verbs at work – Smartkids
- 'How to be brilliant at' series – Brilliant Publications
- Contraction Bingo – Smartkids
- Sentifix – Philip & Tacey

Structure and Rules: Phonology

Observed Behaviours:

- Unintelligible speech
- Difficulties blending sounds
- Substitutes or misses sounds from words
- Difficulties with phonological awareness activities – rhyming, syllable segmentation etc.

General Principles

27 Where possible liaise with the speech and language therapist if a child is known to the speech and language therapy service. There is often a programme of work that could be supported or reinforced in class.

28 Adopt a systematic approach to developing phonological awareness skills to include rhyming, syllable segmentation and auditory discrimination skills.

Communication Techniques for Practitioners

29 Do not pretend to understand a pupil if he/she is unintelligible. They usually know, and this makes them feel that what they have to say is not important. Rather, ask for a repetition, using different words; this way the pupil knows he/she is worth communicating with.

30 Try not to ask pupils to repeat sounds back to you 'correctly'. This will have little long-term effect. For example, if as an adult you were asked to repeat the word 'loch' with a Scottish accent, you would have little difficulty; however, if asked to pronounce the same 'ch' sound in other words every time the 'ck' sound occurred, you would find it extremely difficult.

31 Encourage pupils to listen to your model and emphasise the target sound; e.g. pupil says, 'Look it's a nake', teacher replies, 'Yes it's a sssssnake'.

General Strategies

32 Encourage pupils to use visual support to ensure that they can be effective when communicating. A simple board with key vocabulary (pictures and words) for specific times of the day can be used so the pupil can point to the pictures while talking.

33 Spend as much time as possible on developing a sense of rhythm. Start with very simple single beats using clapping, tapping, shakers etc. There are many tapes of simple rhythm tunes to clap along with, but also use names, one beat per syllable. It may be necessary to hold the pupil's hands and clap along with him/her for quite a long time until he/she can manage alone.

Specific Strategies

34 Play 'Where's That Noise?' – blindfold the pupil, and, using a shaker or something similar, move to different locations in the room and make a noise. The pupil has to point in the direction of the sound. This can be extended to the use of different sounds as well as locations.

35 Use the Language Master for sound discrimination work: make up a pack of percussion instruments and record them in various sequences onto a Language Master card. For example, one beat each of: drum, drum, bells, drum. The pupil listens, then either records the same sequence on the pupil track or records just the odd one out. It is important that this exercise is simple. Gradually expand the idea to include spotting the odd one out in a group of phonic sounds and rhyming words.

36 Again, using the Language Master, record different instruments: pupils can sort into same/different, high/low, loud/soft etc.

37 Play auditory discrimination games such as Sound Lotto (LDA) or tape the voices of the children in the group. Play back the tape and point to the correct child as their voice, giggle etc. is heard. Do the same with members of staff, calling out their names or pointing to their photographs. Familiar sounds around the school can also be recorded and linked to pictures either cut from catalogues or taken with a digital camera, e.g. guillotine, fire alarm, sports whistle etc.

38 Use a screen to play guessing games: the teacher or pupil could stand behind a screen, which hides a set of percussion instruments. These are played and the rest of the class responds by description, e.g. high, low, loud, scratchy, soft, etc.

39 Different sets of cards for the Language Master could be made for matching by sound, rhyming or picking the odd word out. The pupil records the work on the pupil track or writes it down.

40 Play clapping games such as starting a simple clapping rhythm and each pupil joins in, in turn, until everyone is clapping the same rhythm, rather like 'Chinese Whispers'.

41 Play 'Initial Sound Rhythm' by starting children off with a simple sound rhythm, using the same initial sound or initial blend, e.g. 'click-clack-clock'. Pupils then use the same rhythm but change the initial sound or blend, e.g. 'slick-slack-slock', doing this in turn around the circle. To make this easier to start with, give each child a card with an initial sound or blend on it so that they only have to think of changing and blending in the initial sound and keeping the same rhythm. Pupils who find this difficult may need to join in with an able pupil to start with.

42 Develop auditory discrimination skills by using a set of large pictures that illustrate single-syllable words with voiced and unvoiced initial blends, e.g. a key, a bee. In pantomime style, hold up the picture of the key and say, 'Is this some tea?', to which the class replies, 'No, it's a key'. Or, while holding up a picture of a bee, say, 'Is this a pea?', etc. Extend this to include word endings, e.g. 'Is this some soup?', 'No it's a suit', etc.

43 Play a game where the teacher says the sound and the pupil points to a picture of an object beginning with that sound. Choose sounds that are similar, e.g. m/n.

Commercially Available Material

- Sound Beginnings – LDA
- Listen, Think & Do 1 – LDA
- Starter Stile Noisy Lotto – LDA
- Picture Sound Lotto – LDA
- Ice-cream Party – LDA
- Cosmic Critters – LDA
- Sounds Fun at Play – LDA
- Look Hear! – LDA
- Find the Rhyme – LDA
- Ladybug Ladybug – LDA
- Rhyme Lotto – LDA
- Silly Bulls – Philip & Tacey
- Soundaround – David Fulton Publishers
- Early Listening Skills – Winslow
- Rhyme Time – Winslow

Social Communication Skills

Observed Behaviours:

- Poor eye contact
- Difficulties taking turns in conversation
- Makes irrelevant comments or asks inappropriate questions
- Interrupts conversations or changes the topic of conversation rapidly
- Uses inappropriate volume, intonation or unusual voice
- Laughs at the wrong time or appears rude/cheeky
- Tends to talk at people rather than to them
- May take on an adult role
- Finds it difficult to understand jokes or sarcasm
- Struggles to understand implied meaning

General Principles

1 Do not assume anything. Constantly check understanding, especially in social situations.

2 Make rules explicit and model appropriate skills. Use peers as role models. Consistently identify what the pupil should do and record rules visually.

Communication Techniques for Practitioners

3 Do not follow tangential replies – redirect the pupil back to the current topic of conversation. Signal changes in topic, e.g. 'We're now going to talk about the Romans'.

4 Before questioning the pupil's behaviour, check that the instruction given was not ambiguous and that the child's reaction was merely a response to a literal interpretation, e.g. teacher tells pupil to put the writing underneath the picture – meaning 'below'. Pupil lifts stuck-down picture up, puts writing underneath it and sticks picture on top – very frustrating, as the pupil was only doing what he/she was told.

5   It is more helpful to the pupil to say 'The rule is. . .' rather than 'I want you to. . .' or 'You must. . .'.

6   Teach pupils to take responsibility for not understanding: encourage them to have the confidence to tell you if they a) couldn't hear, b) didn't understand the words you used, c) that you were speaking too quickly, etc.

7   Distract and praise appropriate behaviour rather than draw attention to inappropriate behaviour.

8   Simplify language, particularly within cause-and-effect situations, e.g. 'You hit John, he feels sad'.

9   Use 'Responsive Listening' to help develop children's understanding and awareness of emotions and feelings words by very calmly 'echoing' what the distressed pupil's emotion appears to be, for example, if a pupil is obviously feeling sad, say 'You're feeling sad'.

10   Be careful when joking or using sarcasm, you may be taken literally. Make sure you give the literal meaning when using ambiguous language.

General Strategies

11   Work on understanding rules of games. Ensure that children with poor memory and sequencing skills have the opportunity to learn the rules of games thoroughly even if on a one-to-one or small group basis.

12   Have regular joke-telling sessions. Make a cardboard TV screen: pupils take it in turns to tell jokes from the screen at the end of each day.

13   Spend time discussing situations. 'Why do we do this and not that?' 'Why don't we always tell the truth?', etc.

14   Confirm that you have heard what the pupil has said positively; they may not understand 'Mm' or a nod.

15   Give the child a designated place to sit on the carpet.

16   Use apparatus as often as possible to make the intangible tangible, e.g. very simple timetables that can be coloured in to show the passage of time;

arrows on the desk to show the direction of print/order of events. This is done by using coloured adhesive tape to divide the desk into three spaces, left to right, for 'before', 'now', 'later'/'first', 'second', 'third', etc.

17 Help other children in the class to understand that when a pupil is 'telling tales' or sticking to rules too rigorously, this is something he/she has difficulty with, and their support is needed to help him/her sort out what is socially acceptable and what is not.

Specific Strategies

18 Establish a home–school link book so that misunderstandings about 'news time', homework, dates, school rules, peer relationships etc. can be kept to a minimum. Make sure this book records only factual information; do not use it to comment on the pupil's behaviour. Both home and school should record information to share.

19 Consider adult support, it may be needed during unstructured times, such as playtime, lunchtime, some art and craft activities or fact-finding sessions in science, maths, etc., as this can cause great anxiety and therefore a display of inappropriate behaviour.

20 Provide the pupil with a regular, important job to do to help increase his/her feelings of worth. Choose one that is not open-ended nor relies on peer relationships to start with, and then gradually build in some interaction with other members of the class.

21 Prepare the pupil for changes in routine using a visual timetable or task management board (see 'Attention and Listening' strategies 9 and 12).

22 Introduce group rules during small group work, identifying key social communication skills to be developed. For instance, good listening, waiting for a turn to speak and looking at the speaker.

23 Use cue cards (photographs or pictures) to remind children of rules, e.g. interrupting, taking turns, using eye contact.

24 Play turn-taking games, for example rolling a ball, stacking bricks, board games etc.

25 Start small group work with a social communication skills game each day.

26 Introduce 'Special Talk Time' – the opportunity for a child or group of children to talk about their favourite topics of conversation at a specified time during the day.

27 Introduce 'Social Stories' (Gray 2002) to help children understand situations, how to respond and to behave.

28 Use feelings cue cards to develop understanding and use of vocabulary related to feelings/emotions.

29 Set up a social communication skills group to focus on the development of specific social communication skills. Ensure children have opportunities to generalise skills in context by setting targets that can be supported by the class teacher and the child's parents. Use commercially available programmes such as Time to Talk or Socially Speaking (LDA).

30 Use role-play to practise the use of communication skills in specific social situations, for instance practising greetings, initiating conversations or giving a compliment.

31 Consider opportunities to develop social communication skills on the playground by setting up small group games. Teach playground games from the Positive Play programme (LDA).

32 Use dressing-up clothes to focus on 'being someone else'. It may help to put 'oneself into another's shoes'.

33 Play 'soundtrack' music and discuss the feelings that are aroused. Play different instruments and make different sounds – how do these make us feel?

34 Discuss how communication changes according to where you are/who you are talking to. Visit role-play settings that require different language styles, e.g. church, library, restaurant, supermarket etc.

35 Practise simple sentences with different voices and emphasis.

36 Develop the use of mime and gesture in small groups using games such as 'Charades for Kids' (Paul Lamond Toys and Games).

Commercially Available Material

- Feelings Cue Cards – Language for Learning
- Special Talk Time – Language for Learning
- Time to Talk and Socially Speaking – LDA
- Circle Time resources – LDA
- Emotions photo cards – LDA
- Sentimage – LDA
- What would you do? – LDA
- Why? . . . because – LDA
- What's wrong? – LDA
- Positive Play – LDA
- TalkAbout – Speechmark
- Mr/Miss Face – Speechmark
- CLIP Pragmatics – Harcourt Assessment
- Mystifying Metaphors and Smiley Similes – BirdArt
- Good Listening, Good Talking and Good Waiting posters – TaskMaster
- Positive Pragmatic Game Boards – TaskMaster
- Charades for Kids – Paul Lamond Toys and Games

Memory Skills

Observed Behaviours:

- Forgets instructions
- Gets lost within an activity
- Appears non-compliant
- Is unable to recall information or instructions

General Principles for Supporting Memory

1 We tend to remember best what we learn at the beginning and end of a lesson. Maximise on this by creating breaks that provide several beginnings and endings and repeat the main teaching points at these times.

2 Build in revising and recalling with fun activities such as word definition games, word searches and group cartoon drawings related to the topic.

3 Support pupils by teaching techniques that aid memory; that it is their responsibility to remember, e.g. making lists, drawing key points, learning a mnemonic.

Communication Techniques for Teachers and Teaching Assistants

4 Simplify language, speak slowly and introduce new words gradually.

5 Avoid or explain non-literal language.

6 Use the 10-second Rule to allow pupils processing time (see 'Attention and Listening' strategy 3).

7 Use gesture to support verbal language.

Specific Strategies

8 Encourage instant recall by asking pupils to repeat exactly what you have said. Gradually build in longer and longer time delays.

9 Work on taking messages to other members of the class then out of the classroom to another teacher or the school secretary.

10 Practise remembering the key points by counting on fingers, rehearsing and visualising what has to be done.

11 Play Kim's Game (arranging objects/pictures on the table; child looks away while something is removed, child has to say what it is).

12 Use mind maps as these present a wealth of information in a memorable format, particularly if the child is a visual learner. Provide wall size mind maps of the current class topic to act as a reminder when recapping on past lessons and to develop word association skills.

13 Teach auditory and visual mnemonics, for example remembering the colours of the rainbow by initial sound – '<u>R</u>ichard of <u>Y</u>ork <u>g</u>ave <u>b</u>attle <u>in</u> <u>v</u>ain' for red, orange, yellow, green, blue, indigo and violet.

14 Play variations of 'I went to market and I bought. . .'. Using real objects or pictures and changing the situation, e.g. pupils can be Roman soldiers preparing for battle by saying 'I am going to wear . . .' etc.

15 Give pupils a variety of routines and sequences to practise so that memory is improved, e.g. barn dancing, through repetitive movement increases the ability to remember longer and longer dance sequences.

16 Teach rhymes that help pupils remember basic concepts such as how many days there are in the month – 'Thirty days hath September . . .' etc.

17 For remembering words (word finding) help pupils to store words efficiently by working on word association. Look in the 'Understanding the Meaning of Words' strategy section for a range of word definition/sorting and classifying activities.

18 Provide task management boards – see 'Attention and Listening' strategy 12.

19 Provide visual timetables – see 'Attention and Listening' strategy 9.

20 Provide timetables that incorporate what has to be remembered from home such as swimming things on Tuesdays, library books on Wednesdays etc.

21 Encourage pupils to say key points out loud, then whisper them, then 'think' them.

22 Provide prompt cards with a) basic facts such as address, date of birth, days of the week, numbers and spellings of numbers, months of the year, tables etc. and b) main points of discussion.

23 Provide placemats on the desk with the above information.

24 Draw cartoon strips or write colour-coded lists on the whiteboard with key information about the topic in hand.

25 Encourage pupils to take responsibility for using external memories such as lists, key words, mind maps and cartoon strips.

Commercially Available Material

- Mind Maps for Kids – Thorsons
- Developing Alert Listening Skills – Winslow
- The Language Gap – AMS Educational

Speech

Observed Behaviours:

- Difficulties understanding the child
- Speech deteriorates when excited or nervous
- The beginnings and endings of words are omitted
- Syllables in polysyllabic words are left out
- Has difficulty speaking clearly while talking at length

General Principles

1 It is difficult to offer activities in school that benefit children who experience specific speech problems. However, the following ideas can be put into practice to benefit all children. Seek advice from the local speech and language therapy service about the difficulties experienced by individual pupils and their needs in school.

2 Try not to single out children with articulation problems to practise sounds; this is unhelpful and can hinder progress. 'Sound' work is better done in small groups or with the whole class, e.g. 'Jolly Phonics', 'I-Spy' (using sounds not letter names) and alliteration work, e.g. <u>B</u>obby <u>b</u>ursts <u>b</u>lue <u>b</u>alloons with <u>B</u>ecky.

3 Deal with teasing from classmates positively, so that pupils' self-esteem does not suffer.

Communication Techniques for Practitioners

4 Do not pretend to understand a pupil if he/she is unintelligible. They usually know, and this makes them feel that what they have to say is not important. Rather, ask for a repetition, using different words; this way the pupil knows he/she is worth communicating with.

5 Confirm that you have understood what has been said by saying things like, 'Oh, so you spent the evening with Granny', etc. This relaxes the pupil and gives him/her the confidence to continue.

6   Make sure that the pupil in question can see how you speak. Face the child, encourage him/her to look at your mouth and speak slowly and clearly.

7   Try not to ask the pupil to repeat sounds back to you 'correctly'. This will have little long-term effect. For example, if as an adult you were asked to repeat the word 'loch' with a Scottish accent, you would have little difficulty. However, if asked to pronounce the same 'ch' sound in other words every time the 'ck' sound occurred, you would find it extremely difficult.

General Strategies

8   Encourage pupils to use visual support to ensure that he/she can be effective when communicating. A simple board with key vocabulary (pictures and words) for specific times of the day can be used so the pupil can point to the pictures while talking.

9   Keep classroom noise to a minimum whenever possible.

10   Do not expect a pupil to be able to produce a sound spontaneously that he/she has been taught to say in isolation. For example, a child who had just learnt to produce the sound 'k' went to her speech and language therapy session and said, 'I touldn't tay "t" before tould I? But I tan now, listen: "k"'.

11   Where possible liaise with the speech and language therapist if a pupil in your class attends speech and language therapy. There is often a programme of work that could be supported or reinforced in school.

12   Play 'Straw Carry' with pieces of paper and strong straws. The pupil holds the straw in his/her mouth and places the other end on a small piece of paper. Without touching the paper, he/she sucks the straw so that his/her breath draws the paper against it. He/she then tries to walk to another part of the room without dropping the paper. This can also be played with a group of children as a relay race.

13 Play 'Straw Polo', which is like blow football. The pupil blows a ping-pong ball along through a straw. Races can be set up to see who crosses the finishing line first. Variations on this can be blowing paper boats across water, blow-paint pictures, blowing bubbles etc.

14 Sing songs or play games that involve pretending to eat, e.g. 'This is the way we chew our gum, chew our gum'.

15 Licking exercise such as licking a lolly or pretending to lick jam or honey from around the mouth using the tongue only.

16 Tell 'Mr Tongue Stories'; the children make their tongue do what Mr Tongue is doing in the story; e.g. Mr Tongue goes for a walk all round his garden – the children put out their tongues and make them go round without touching their lips – then Mr Tongue goes back in this house and walks all round that – the children run their tongues over their back and front teeth, etc.

17 Use the sounds 'oo', 'ee' and 'ah' in an exaggerated manner either as the noise characters make in a story or as a refrain in a song. The aim is to exercise the muscles around the mouth rather than to practise the accuracy of the sounds.

18 Play 'Sound Lotto' (see Attention and Listening strategy 22) but encourage the pupils to copy the relevant sounds before putting the counter on the correct picture.

19 Link sounds to percussion instruments, e.g. <u>b</u>ang, <u>b</u>ang as the drum is hit, <u>t</u>ing, <u>t</u>ing as the triangle is hit and <u>m</u>ack, <u>m</u>ack as the maracas are played etc.

20 Play 'Find Your Fish' using pictures that help children to practise sounds they are having difficulty with, e.g fish, dish, shell, shoe, sheep, etc.

Commercially Available Material

- Schubi Mimic – TaskMaster
- Sound Lotto – LDA
- Find Your Fish – Philip & Tacey

Glossary

Terminology and jargon can be very confusing. This chapter provides a glossary of terms often found in specialist reports.

Articulation	Control of speech organs in order to produce speech sounds.
Articulatory/verbal dyspraxia	A motor-programming disorder, which involves difficulties in programming the sequence of movements required to produce continuous speech.
Asperger's syndrome	An autism spectrum disorder first described by Hans Asperger, characterised by social interaction difficulties, all-absorbing narrow interests, the need for routine and motor clumsiness.
Attention control	The ability to maintain focus.
Attention deficit (hyperactivity) disorder	A difficulty where the child is easily distracted. Hyperactivity is where the child shows high levels of restlessness as well.
Auditory discrimination	The ability to hear the difference in sounds.
Auditory memory	The ability to remember information that is heard.
Autistic spectrum disorder	Children with an autism spectrum disorder experience impairments of social interaction, social communication and imagination. An autism spectrum disorder is a lifelong developmental disability.
Bilingual	Two languages being developed simultaneously.
Cleft lip	A split in the upper lip, which occurs during foetal development, usually associated with cleft palate.

Cleft palate	A structural abnormality whereby the roof of the mouth is not formed properly, causing problems with eating, breathing, articulation and hearing. Often occurs with a split upper lip (cleft lip).
Conductive hearing loss	A hearing impairment caused by a difficulty in transmitting sound through the outer or middle ear.
Delayed language development	Language development follows the normal sequence and pattern but at a slower rate.
Disordered language development	Language development does not follow the normal pattern, giving rise to complex language problems in one or more specific areas of language.
Down's syndrome	A chromosomal abnormality often causing considerable learning difficulties including speech and language problems.
Dysarthria	A difficulty caused by damage to the central nervous system (neurological), which results in loss of muscle control for speech.
Dysfluency	A difficulty in producing smooth, fluent speech. This term includes stammering (UK) / stuttering (USA).
Echolalia	The repetition of words of phrases heard without understanding. Echolalia can be delayed or immediate.
Expressive language	The use of spoken language to convey a message.
Fluctuating hearing loss	Caused when children suffer from repeated colds or catarrhal infections, often undetected as child is 'clear' at the time of hearing check, but can have a significant effect on language development.
Fragile X syndrome	The bottom tip of an x chromosome is broken off so that it appears fragile. Characteristics of this chromosomal abnormality include learning difficulties, social communication problems and language difficulties.
Global development delay	The child experiences a delay in all areas of development.

Grommets	Small plastic tubes that keep open incisions surgically made in the eardrum to ventilate the inner ear, helping to prevent inner ear infection.
Intonation	The rising and falling pitch patterns of language that express a wide range of meaning.
Language Master	A simple portable audio/visual device using cards striped with magnetic tape to provide auditory and visual information simultaneously.
Mnemonic	An aid to memory, e.g. initial letters of a sentence to spell a word or a picture accompanying a word.
Morphology	The way in which word structures change to signal a change in meaning, e.g. sleep, sleeping, slept, asleep.
Otitis media	The most common form of conductive hearing loss, caused by catarrhal infections spreading to the middle ear via the eustachian tube.
Phoneme	The individual sounds we use when pronouncing sounds. There are approximately forty in the English language.
Phonology	The speech sound system of a language – the rules that govern how sounds are organised in words in order to convey different meanings.
Phonological delay	The child's phonological development follows a typical pattern, but at a slower rate. Phonological processes appear to persist beyond the age at which they should disappear.
Phonological disorder	The child's phonological development does not follow a typical pattern of development, i.e. phonological processes that do not occur during typical development are present.
Pragmatics	The use of language in social situations, including conversational skills and the understanding and use of non-verbal communication.

119

Prosody	The melody of language determined by pitch and loudness, speed and rhythm.
Receptive language	Understanding spoken language.
Sally Anne Test/Smartie Tube Test	Simple tests devised by Uta Frith (1989) to assess theory of mind.
Selective mutism	The child does not speak in certain situations, e.g. school, but can speak in others, e.g. home. Often psychological in origin.
Semantic pragmatic disorder	Historically this term has been used to describe children with specific semantic and pragmatic difficulties. Children with semantic pragmatic disorder are now described as experiencing an autism spectrum condition.
Semantics	The meaning of words and sentences.
Sensori-neural hearing loss	Severe deafness as a result of damage to the inner ear or nerve pathways to the brain.
Signalong	A system of hand shapes and movements that relate to the spoken grammatical form of English and can therefore be used to illustrate what the speaker is saying.
Social communication skills	See pragmatics.
Stammering (stuttering)	See dysfluency.
Syntax	The rule system that governs the structure of language at a word, phrase and sentence level.
Theory of mind	Awareness that others have different thoughts, feelings and knowledge from yourself.

References

Buzan, T. (2003) *Mind Maps for Kids*. London: Thorsons.

DfEE (2001) *Supporting the Target Setting Process*. Nottingham: DFEE.

DfES (2001a) *Special Educational Needs: Code of Practice*. London: HMSO.

DfES (2001b) *SEN: Toolkit*. London: HMSO.

DfES (2004) *Speaking, Listening and Learning: Working with Children in Key Stages 1 & 2*. Norwich: HMSO.

Frith, U. (1989) *Autism: Explaining the Enigma*. Oxford: Basil Blackwell.

Gray, C. (2002) *My Social Stories Book*. London: Jessica Kingsley.

Hayden, S. (1996) *Speaking and Listening: Stage One* and *Speaking and Listening: Stage Two*. Hereford and Worcester County Council.

Hayden, S. and Jordan. E. (2000) *Language for Learning across the Curriculum*. Kidderminster: Language for Learning.

Johnson, M. (2001) *Functional Language in the Classroom (and at Home)*. Clinical Communication Materials, Manchester Metropolitan University.

Law, J., Lindsay, G. and Pearcey, N. *et al.* (2000) *Provision for Children with Speech and Language Needs in England and Wales: Facilitating Communication between Education and Health Services*. Nottingham: DfEE.

Martin, D. (2000) *Teaching Children with Speech and Language Difficulties*. London: David Fulton Publishers.

QCA (1999) *The National Curriculum: Handbook for Primary Teachers in England*. London: QCA.

Ripley, K., Barrett, J. and Fleming, P. (2001) *Inclusion for Children with Speech and Language Impairments*. London: David Fulton Publishers.

Speake, J. (2003) *How to Identify and Support Children with Speech and Language Difficulties*. Wisbech: LDA.

Tilstone, C. (1998) *Observing Teaching and Learning: Principles into Practice*. London: David Fulton Publishers.

Appendix 1: Suppliers of Commercially Available Material

Supplier	Address	Telephone
AMS Educational	Woodside Trading Estate, Low Lane, Horsforth, Leeds, LS18 5NY	0113 258 0309
BirdArt	46 St Peter's Drive, Martley, Worcestershire, WR6 6QZ	01886 888151
Black Sheep Press	67 Middleton, Cowling, Keighley, West Yorkshire, BD22 0DQ	01535 631 346
Brilliant Publications	The Old School Yard, Leighton Road, Northall, Dunstable, Bedfordshire, LU6 2HA	01525 229720
David Fulton Publishers	2 Park Square, Milton Park, Abingdon, Oxford OX14 4RN	020 7017 6000
Drake Educational Associates	St Fagan's Road, Fairwater, Cardiff, CF5 3AE	029 2056 0333
Harcourt Assessment *Previously known as The Psychological Corporation*	Halley Court, Jordan Hill, Oxford, OX2 8EJ	01865 888188
Language for Learning	Speech & Language Centre, Franche Clinic, Marlpool Place, Kidderminster, Worcestershire, DY11 5BB	01562 751866
LDA	Duke Street, Wisbech, Cambs, PE13 2AE	01945 463441
Living and Learning (usually available through LDA)	5-7 Pembroke Avenue, Waterbeach, Cambridge, CB5 9QP	01223 864886

Supplier	Address	Telephone
Paul Lamond Toys & Games Ltd (available in high street shops)	4 Pate Road, Leicester Road Industrial Estate, Melton Mowbray, Leicestershire, LE13 0RG	Sales@MailOrder Express.com
Philip and Tacey Ltd	North Way, Andover, Hants, SP10 5BA	01264 332171
Questions Publications	Leonard House, 321 Bradford Street, Digbeth, Birmingham, B5 6ET	0121 666 7878
SEMERC	Granada Learning Ltd, Quay Street, Manchester, M60 9EA	0161 827 2927
Smartkids (UK) Ltd	5 Station Road, Hungerford, Berkshire, RG17 0DY	01488 644644
Speechmark	Telford Road, Bicester, Oxon, OX26 4LQ	01869 244 644
STASS Publications	44 North Road, Ponteland, Northumberland, NE20 9UR	01661 822316
TaskMaster Ltd	Morris Road, Leicester, LE2 6BR	0116 270 4286
Thorsons (available in high street bookshops)	HarperCollins Publishers, 77-85 Fulham Palace Road, Hammersmith, London, W6 8JB	020 8741 7070
Widgit Software Ltd	Widgit Sales, 124 Cambridge Science Park, Milton Road, Cambridge, CB4 0ZS	01223 425558
Winslow	Goyt Side Road, Chesterfield, Derbyshire, S40 2PH	0845 921 1777

Appendix 2: Language for Learning

Training Opportunities

Language for Learning offers an extensive range of training options for school staff.

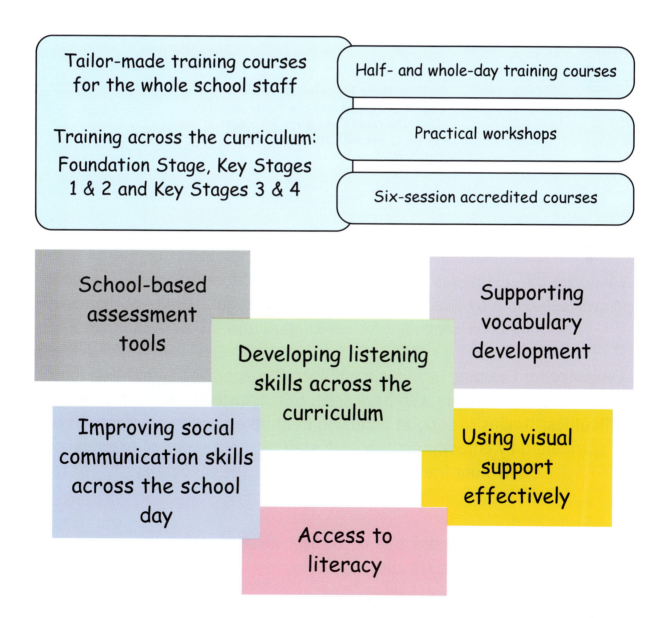

Tailor-made training courses for the whole school staff

Training across the curriculum: Foundation Stage, Key Stages 1 & 2 and Key Stages 3 & 4

Half- and whole-day training courses

Practical workshops

Six-session accredited courses

School-based assessment tools

Developing listening skills across the curriculum

Supporting vocabulary development

Improving social communication skills across the school day

Using visual support effectively

Access to literacy

Feedback from our courses:

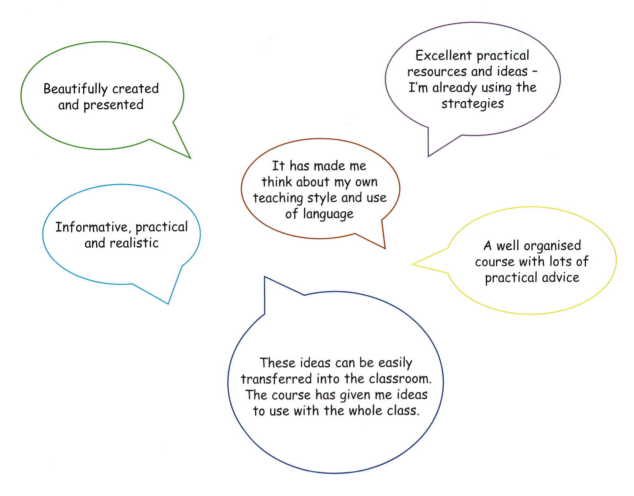

Beautifully created and presented

Excellent practical resources and ideas – I'm already using the strategies

It has made me think about my own teaching style and use of language

Informative, practical and realistic

A well organised course with lots of practical advice

These ideas can be easily transferred into the classroom. The course has given me ideas to use with the whole class.

Language for Learning is a joint health and education initiative developed in Worcestershire by Sue Hayden and Emma Jordan, authors of the award winning book *Language for Learning Across the Curriculum*.

Language for Learning provides a collaborative approach to training those working with children who have speech, language or communication difficulties. It aims to support inclusion of children across all stages of the curriculum by empowering teaching staff to use a range of practical, curriculum-friendly strategies across the school day.

For more information, contact us on 01562 751866

Language for Learning, Speech & Language Centre, Franche Clinic, Marlpool Place, Kidderminster, Worcestershire, DY11 5BB

Training at Key Stages 1 & 2

LANGUAGE for **LEARNING**
supporting pupils with communication difficulties

Language for Learning offers an extensive range of training options for school staff.

Identifying your needs ...

Suitable sessions ...

Do you want a whole school approach from assessment to choosing strategy ideas, including assessment, links to the curriculum and strategy planning?

You need → 'Language for Learning Across the Curriculum'

Do you want to developing listening skills across Key Stages 1 & 2? Need support differentiating the new Speaking, Listening & Learning curriculum?

You need → 'Developing Listening Skills Across the Curriculum'

Do you want a language to talk about language? Would you like a guide to speech, language and communication skills, terminology and identification tools?

You need → 'Introductory Session'

Do you want to improve listening skills and pupils' ability to follow instructions in the classroom?

You need → 'Processing Instructions & Information'

Do you want to develop vocabulary skills and plan vocabulary development across the curriculum?

You need → 'Understanding the Meaning of Words'

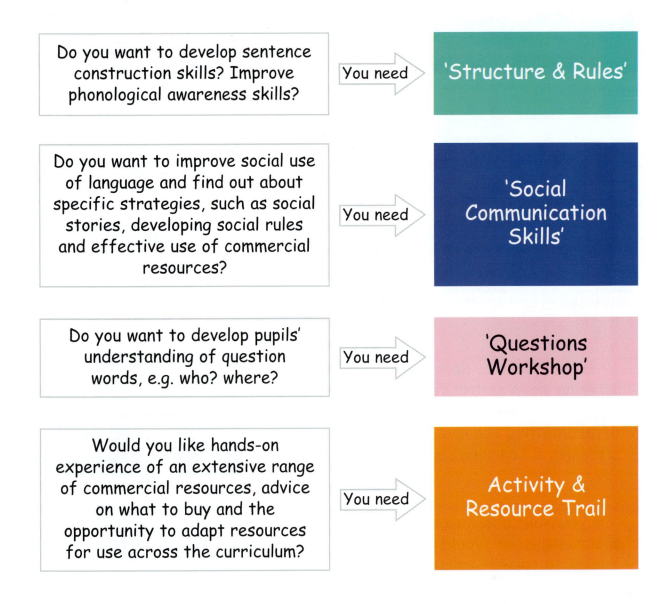

Do you want to develop sentence construction skills? Improve phonological awareness skills?	You need	'Structure & Rules'
Do you want to improve social use of language and find out about specific strategies, such as social stories, developing social rules and effective use of commercial resources?	You need	'Social Communication Skills'
Do you want to develop pupils' understanding of question words, e.g. who? where?	You need	'Questions Workshop'
Would you like hands-on experience of an extensive range of commercial resources, advice on what to buy and the opportunity to adapt resources for use across the curriculum?	You need	Activity & Resource Trail

All courses listed above are halfday or twilight sessions.
Combine them for a whole day.

For more information, contact us on 01562 751866

Language for Learning, Speech & Language Centre,
Franche Clinic, Marlpool Place, Kidderminster,
Worcestershire, DY11 5BB

supporting pupils with communication difficulties